Table of Contents

Barracking from the Sidelines 2017

(My personal political commentary on politicians and political events in 2017)

By Greg Tuck

Preface

Australian Politics

Dominated by a federal government, in a three-tier system of government, Australian politics is based on a constitution written in the 1890's that is extremely difficult to change via referendums. It is a Westminster system of government that has two separate chambers that are dominated by two major parties whose ideologies differ and both the sides are very combative to the extent that agreement on issues except politician wage increase, are hard won battles. If one side thinks of an idea, the other side shoots it down in flames, whether the idea is good or not. The public have become disillusioned and feel impotent to change things and see most politicians as merely sucking on the public teat and lining their own pockets. A good few of the political rank's behaviour does nothing to dispel that idea.

Politics changed a lot in Australia from late 2013 onwards, although many will attest to the fact that it hasn't changed at all. There are still lies, deception, obfuscation and manipulation and these have had to become more sophisticated as social media has come to the fore. I have been adding my own comments to mainstream media and my own political blog in those years and on reflection I am amazed at the types of characters that are regularly unearthed and come to the forefront in our political climate.

Some characters have developed over that time. Some were just fleeting shadows on the political spectrum. Others rose from obscurity and some may have also have faded back into it. Characters and events overlap. Views change and political manoeuvres take place. Ideology dictates much of what goes on. Hopefully my blog entries and reflections will help paint a picture of these characters and events that dominated the political scene in this period. This is not a chronological history of the time, merely one person's thoughts that he wanted to scream at the major players in Australian politics at the time.

However, the disappointing thing about all these comments and research is what I still really don't understand is, how does the Canberra bubble still remain intact with so many pricks in it? Are there special properties of moral vacuums?

January

- Federal Government backbencher Tony Abbott calls for Australia to relocate its embassy in Israel from Tel Aviv to Jerusalem
- Federal Health Minister Sussan Ley stands aside while travel claims are being investigated
- Automated debt recovery system for welfare overpayments (Robodebt) comes under fire
- The Federal Government announces a long-awaited overhaul of MP's travel entitlements.
- Former One Nation Senator Rod Culleton loses his Senate seat weeks after the Federal Court of Australia declares him bankrupt
- Severe storms hit Queensland leaving 1,500 homes without power and causes floods in suburbs of Brisbane and Ipswich.
- Prime Minister Malcolm Turnbull reshuffles his Cabinet for the fourth time since taking office
- Malcolm Turnbull announces that US President Donald Trump has confirmed that he will honour the refugee swap deal with Australia as agreed by the Obama administration.
- The Federal Government announces plans to review child care and to cut family tax benefits.
- Donald Trump, is sworn in as the 45th President of the United States

Instead of sending troops, can't the leaders of countries challenge each other on Masterchef?

We may be blaming Islam but remind me how many Crusades took place in the Middle East? The only thing that's changed is the weapons used.

Australia's involvement in Iraq, Afghanistan and Vietnam achieved as much as the please slow down sign at the Tour De France.

"How ironic that in a place that survives almost solely on hot air and wind, Parliament House in Canberra; that solar and wind generated power are to be cut by the government from any Clean Energy Finance Corporation funding. I wonder if Coal has been added to the CEFC funding categories. We dig out environmentally polluting coal and bury common sense. What must the world think of us?"

"War, what is it good for?" The answer isn't absolutely nothing. It provides a ready market for munitions manufacturers. It allows countries to spend money on defence and less on health, education, medicine and alleviating poverty. It allows governments to maintain a security alert and thus keep the populace living in fear and them in power. What has Australia gained from its war in Vietnam, Afghanistan, Iraq and on terrorism except photo opportunities for politicians in flak jackets?

With the Aussie dollar so low, is it the best time to sell the farm?

Get the elected representative to represent their electorate's views not just their party's views. That might help.

They have effectively taken the pea out of the whistle for whistle-blowers.

If there are no asylum seekers coming, why do we have the new prohibitive bans on doctors etc.?

Both parties are anti-asylum seekers. Let's face it.

Under Australian law asylum seekers are criminals. Under International law they are not.

Is a white paper a racist thing?

Take note Australia. People lose dignity when they become poorer.

There is a cultural, economic and social divide that is actively being encouraged by our government. They want us to castigate and condemn as a first course of action rather than lend a hand. We are now living a lot closer to each other in this shrinking world, but have never been more apart; and as we become more civilized, we have become less civil. Are our children being encouraged to grow up in a moral and ethical vacuum?

So, the person who is currently in the Speaker's or President's chair can better represent their electorate and also to remove any perceived bias of the Speaker of The House of Representatives or by the President of the Senate would each position be better filled by an independent member of the judiciary?

What are the roles and responsibilities of Independent Commissions, the Parliament and the Judiciary in providing good governance?

February

- Malcolm Turnbull admits that he donated $1.75 million to the Liberal Party for the last election.
- Treasurer Scott Morrison brings a lump of coal into the House of Representatives saying "This is coal. Don't be afraid, don't be scared."
- The Washington Post reports that US President Donald Trump berated Malcolm Turnbull during a phone call which Trump dubbed his "worst call by far". The pair discussed the "dumb" refugee deal between Australia and the Obama administration, before he abruptly ended the call. This seems to contradict what Turnbull had previously said.
- Senator Corey Bernardi quits the Liberal Party to form a new political party, the Australian Conservatives
- North Korea test fires a ballistic missile across the Sea of Japan.

How the liberal voters in South Australia must be clapping and cheering their second on the ticket senator. Their voices are being represented by....... oh that is right.... being represented by one less person now.

The arrival of a new conservative party can't come soon enough. We have been trapped in a 1950's time warp.

"Now Mal can move to the left.
As Cory steps to the right.
Always shooting from the hips.
Seeking the limelight.
For his right wing thrust
Was driving us insane
Let's end his Time Warp game."

This legislation is not about caring for children it is about making it even more difficult for people to access childcare. Families facing rising house prices need to have two wage earners to try to get a deposit. Kill the need for that and then perhaps the childcare costs will not eat into the budget as much. As usual politicians turn their backs on an issue as the photo poignantly points out.

Can we please have a cap on lots of other things: politician's perks, Dorothy Dix questions in Question Time, Donald Trump headlines, door stop press conferences, three-word slogans, repeating words and phrases such as jobs, jobs, jobs.

Malcolm says, "the honourable thing for Cory to do is to resign". Yet even though they are addressed as 'Honourable', when was the last honourable thing that a politician ever did? Perhaps it was way back in 1971 when John Gorton voted himself out of the job as PM.

Seems that a number of politicians have swapped sides over the years. They find themselves on a carousel and want to be the lead horse, not recognising that there is no lead horse. Benedict Arnold, Cassius, Guy Fawkes, Philby, Burgess and McLean, Vidkun Quisling and Judas Iscariot and our home grown, Meg Lees and Cheryl Kernot. Cory Bernardi has just been added to the list.

Can't wait for the Bernardi manifesto. We will finally know what he stands for. As for Turnbull's, Malcolm is continually rewriting his on a daily basis.

They may talking about rats leaving a sinking ship but while they are on board they rock the boat and it is in danger of capsizing as well as going way off course.

What did Cory learn at the United Nations? Not how to unite a nation obviously.

Amazing how some members of parliamentarians find the stylized put downs of others, humorous. We have far better comedic talent in

Australia who don't need to resort to such devices to get a laugh out of an audience. The sad thing is that these comedians are regularly unemployed whilst wanna-be comedians in Canberra get paid megabucks to fall short of the mark by a long way.

Go the policy and not the person and maybe you gain credibility, but right now Malcolm's credibility seems to be in its final death throes. But how his fan base to the right of the speaker and the right wing of politics love him.

If everything was equitable and fair Malcolm, we would all have Comm cars. We would all have Point Piper mansions. But there is a real difference between rich and poor in Australia and your policies not only entrench that but escalate the divide. We now have the needy and the greedy.

"Whose line will people buy?" Do we now have to buy lines that the politicians put forward? Can we get a deduction if we are hard of hearing? Are we paying by the word because many politicians are so verbose? Have we swapped gold pass perks for bonus payments based on lines of arguments? No wonder our debt is climbing!

Here's a little lurk that got through. An advanced diploma of two and a half year full time study now costs students more than a three year degree even though it is considered of lesser value when it comes to job opportunities. It also has a loan limit of $10,000 rather than the uncapped HECS loans. Students from lower socio-economic groups now can't afford even that entry course into the work environment. Their Health Care card can't be used for fee concessions either on advanced diplomas. The government is effectively reducing the opportunities and range of studies available to students and blocking pathways to those who have just missed out on degree courses.

Should Australia Post boss Ahmed Fahour's $5.6m salary be paid on performance? Can his pay check be sent to him by post? Perhaps he could receive it in the form of stamps.

Here's some questions for Peter Dutton who seems to have gone missing. "If Mohit Ahlawat, aged 21, who has just hammered five consecutive sixes in the final over of his astonishing knock of 300 from 72 balls in a T20 match, arrived in a boat at Christmas Island would he be granted asylum given our recent loss in the Chappell Hadlee trophy series? How quickly would he be processed? Or would he only have a choice of playing for Manus or Nauru.

"So that would allow, you know, potentially plenty of planning time." After a pregnant pause, Christian Porter announced a pregnant pause in the proposed legislation's enactment.

Seems that Christian Porter has expectations for the youth of this country to go to find jobs. Sadly, he doesn't realise that the jobs where these people can afford to live just aren't there. He then expects these people to jump through enormous red-taped hoops to get some support, ignoring the fact that the applications and job hunting required is too onerous, futile and soul destroying. Then he wants to punish them by having a four-week delay in support. At least Marie Antoinette suggested cake not air to live on.

I hope that all politicians read the fine print in the welfare legislation that's about to hit parliament. The problem with such large pieces of legislation for many politicians is that it can divert them away from the more important aspects of being a parliamentarian such as the quality of the chateaubriand beef, the haunting aroma of the decades old cabernet that goes with their meal etc. Many will just probably look at the simple speak version of the legislation and give their nod of approval to changes that will slash support to those who need it the most. then they will look at the dessert menu and make the more difficult choice between baked ricotta cheesecake and creme brulee.

Personally, I think politicians should be grateful for any level of flight that they can get to leave Canberra. A lot of visitors would hang on to the wings just to get out of that soulless place.

What a beastly thing Cory has done. Has he seen the influence that Pauline Hanson has had and begun to think that a raving lunatic outside the party is better than one inside the party? I don't think I like the "look at me!" mentality that pervades politics these days. Too much time spent in front of the cameras and not enough time spent doing what we elected them to do.

They don't call it the COALition for nothing mate.

Let's think logically about this. The opposition are really unable to put their policies into action until after the next election, if they win that. The government is able to implement theirs if it negotiates well. However, in this alternate universe called Canberra, it is the government that spends all its time criticising the opposition's policies. The only benefit in doing that is to hide what they are actually doing or not doing. They would be better off saying what they have achieved rather than what the opposition, if it was in power might achieve. It is not just the people in South Australia who are in the dark, it is the whole nation because they don't know what the government are doing. Come to think of it, perhaps the government don't know what they are doing either.

The way the Whitehouse staff stuff up names, the phone call to join in a new war will go to Austria rather than Australia. Adam Bandt needn't worry.

Senator McDonald must be happy that Mr Turnbull is boosting family support by $20 per week because that may balance out for his family the loss of the gold pass.

If the Labor Party (who is not in power by the way) is starting "an assault on the living standards of Australians", then the government by comparison is going for annihilation.

Perhaps all politicians who enter parliament should get the New Start allowance levels as the only perk/allowance they get. I bet the New Start allowance would not be up for grabs so readily when it comes to budget cuts.

Senator McDonald is absolutely right about not getting paid much..... when you compare it with the boss of Australia Post perhaps. However, when you compare it with the basic wage of Australians, when you compare it with the poverty line threshold, then he could be wrong.

If a hypocrite is an imposter, then a fake hypocrite is the real deal. Not sure you got your word choice right but if so then praising Bill is on your agenda now.

When it comes to TAFE, this government in budget terms sees it likes this. That's A F..... Extravagance. Not sure what the F stands for though.

One wonders how many voting groups will feel marginalised by the policies of this government by the next election? Current young students and unemployed, those who still can't afford houses, pensioners who have had their pensions in real terms cut, students in tertiary education settings facing enormous HECS costs and NOW the most marginalised of all, politicians!

Good on Senator Ian MacDonald! Defending the indefensible is not a crime. It is an indication of ignorance but not a crime.

I can't see the need for derision about millionaires. Given the ballooning housing market prices anyone who owns one is a millionaire.

Not sure about the analogy about Malcolm and a spot changing leopard. He is more like a chameleon. You never see the real person, just the one that blends in with his surroundings. Becomes a right wing liberal when told to. Comes across as a moderate to the public. Has left leaning tendencies to entice Labor voters. And is often found camouflaged sitting on fences.

Peter Dutton wants even more powers to play the role of St Peter at the gates of heaven (Australia). He wants the final say on revalidating visas based on information he may (or may not) have in his possession. Why not just put out an executive order, Peter? Already you have over

1250 people in detention centres on Manus, Nauru and in Australia whom you have put into an unending purgatory. Now you want to send even more back to a living hell they have sought asylum from. With such omnipotent powers you may be tempted to name your own price for entry. After all 30 pieces of silver doesn't go far these days.

Oh, to be a politician. The superannuation is the best in the nation and you don't have to wait until 55 to access it. Free meals. Free flights. Free healthcare. Free accommodation. Freedom to say what you think. How many of us wouldn't mind a little bit of that? Perhaps the Lord Mayor of Melbourne, Robert Doyle, could suggest to the homeless people he wants to get off his streets that they stand for parliament.

MP's get entitlements and allowances but aren't we the voting public entitled to get something more than what we get from them. We are sick of making allowances for their poverty when our own situation is far more desperate.

Malcolm is a self-made man. One wonders how that is physically possible and the images that come to mind aren't great. If he indeed is his own man and stands up to billionaires, where is his courage to stand up to the right wing of his party and look them in the eye and take them on?

Not a good look this morning. Malcolm Turnbull flanked by two men when discussing childcare. Childcare is a parenting responsibility. Some gender balance at his press conference would have more politically correct but there is a dearth of female ministers isn't there? Smacks a little of Tony Abbott being Minister for Women and Trump's signing of an executive order on abortion with only men in the picture.

There won't be a situation where our politicians will be suing each other for character assassination. You can't assassinate what is not there.

What is it with our politicians? The role modelling they exhibit should be called for what it is, completely abhorrent. They expect us to trust and adore them but what they offer in return are childish sledges (with apologies to children) that try to belittle each other. Their skin is so tough that these slings and arrows bounce off, but the message they send to the younger generation is that bullying and lies are okay. If we wish to celebrate success in this country as Mr Joyce suggests, then celebrate what is good in people not what gets under their skin. The sycophants behind the sledgers should not be applauding and cheering but realise the damage that such inane words are doing. It is about time we elected people of character to parliament who will spend more time governing rather than being show ponies (with apologies to ponies).

Barnaby Joyce can hardly argue a case against Barnett because Barnaby's party isn't really a stand-alone party. He is only Deputy PM because his party is aligned with the Liberals and because his party preferences the Liberals. Glasshouses Barnaby!

Will Senator McDonald be retracting his comments about the gold pass once he sees just what the dole payment is that he will be getting after the next election?

Here's a way to get rid of preference deals. First past the post wins in both the Senate and the House of Reps. The majority rules in each electorate if we do that. So many lobbyists and party officiandos may be out of business. Think of the trees that would be saved because how to vote cards would not be needed. We would know the election result on election night! People would not be sucking up to parties they have nothing in common with. The whole idea is too simple and that is why it will never happen.

The omnibus will soon be busted. The trade-offs for child care at the expense of welfare cuts surely won't get passed if common sense prevails...... oh, we are talking politics here; and in Canberra too where common sense and common decency have 'left the building'. There is every chance the omnibus will not run out of steam.

Barnett's philosophy is: "It's not how you play the game, it's whether you win or lose." The game of politics has no rules.

I used to think that my views were pretty mainstream. That climate change did exist and fossil fuels weren't the future. That asylum seekers shouldn't be locked up for long periods in detention centres, particularly on islands overseas. That everyone should have adequate access to healthcare and education. That everyone should be treated equally regardless of gender, disability, socio-economic background, race, religion or gender preference. That there needed to be a safety net for those less fortunate. Apparently, these days these are very leftist views, but I'm staying where I am, hoping that the ship of moral conscience will somehow stop listing to starboard and return to a state of equilibrium.

Is there some sort of dehumanising disease that politicians are exposed to when they first get to Canberra? They arrive with the best of intentions as normal caring individuals, but then go through a strange transformation where their ego inflates and their self-importance readings go through the roof. They arrive professing to know very little and suddenly they seem to know everything about everything. They arrive with a selfless attitude and within days they are horse-trading and saying, "What's in it for me?" Canberra or maybe just Parliament House is a very dangerous place. Perhaps the politicians there should be quarantined in case the dehumanising virus is contagious. The sooner some vaccine is found, the sooner some humanity may return to these sadly afflicted everyday Australians.

The question arises. Is the fence to keep the politicians in? Remember the film "One Flew Over the Cuckoo's Nest". Let's not let them break out!!!!

Surely Mr Fahour's speech could be sent to everyone by mail. Then no-one would ever get to read it. But if he submitted his resignation by mail, he could easily be employed into his nineties.

Georges are in the news today. One wants to step down and one should. Both might soon be in new jobs. One heading overseas and another heading to somewhere further to the right maybe.

Sam Dastyari may be seen as the pot ready to take on the kettle if he gets embroiled in Senate estimates discussion of the lurks and perks of politicians and senior executives of public entities.

Regarding the bromance between Cory and Tony. Can't see them having secret trysts anywhere.

The Oscars' La La Land gaffe may be attributed to Australia Post. The wrong envelope was delivered. And if you're expecting good service from Auspost you would have to be in La La Land.

March

- The Hazelwood Power Station in Victoria was taken off-line, after first coming into operation in 1964
- A heat wave in south-eastern Australia results in record breaking temperatures, bushfires and extensive power loss
- Floods occur in Southern parts of WA
- Severe cyclone hits north and central Queensland causing damage and floods
- Malcolm Turnbull rejects calls to exclude the big four banks from the company tax cuts
- The UN warns that the world is facing the largest humanitarian crisis since World War II, with up to 20 million people at risk of starvation and famine in Yemen, Somalia, South Sudan and Nigeria
- An Islamic terror attack in London, England, kills five people and injures more than fifty others
- Brexit negotiations begin between Britain and the European Union.

No-one listens to Mum and Dad fighting on the chamber floor. The noise is from the kids behind hoping that question time is over and yelling "Are we there yet? Are we there yet?"

Can we please ask the Fair Work Commission to look at the salary and penalty rates (and perks) of politicians? Let Malcolm and co. then tell their colleagues that they had nothing to do with it.

Can we have answer time please and not question time.

Does immigration affect house prices? In comparison to what? Negative gearing? Capital gains provisions? Those two have been dismissed though because changes to them may affect politicians' ability to earn any more. So let's blame the migrants. Why not even go for the asylum seekers as well while we are at it.

Perhaps the Health Estimates will estimate the health of this government before rigor mortis sets in.

I don't get it. The government should be prattling on about its policies and the changes they are making. Instead they are talking about their opponents' policies as if they were still in opposition. What a Bizarro world we live in.

This talk about George Brandis heading to London is a lot of codswallop. There is no plane or boat big enough to carry his bookcase!

Dutton to Cormann: "Is Malcolm out of his depth and drowning and not just waving?"

Cormann to Dutton: " Perhaps; though Tony shouldn't have tried to come to the rescue. Like red speedos to a bull but don't joke. There could be another live microphone. Let's talk about weight loss." Dutton to Cormann: "I was. The sooner we get rid of those two dead weights the better."

Why did a sane law/piece of legislation take so many years to develop? Oh, that's right, we have a parliament where common sense is left in the coat locker in exchange for the mentality that if one side says yes, the opposing side must say no. Get rid of the party system and have some genuine people in parliament please.

Michaelia Cash has been chastised over her pantsuit. Women tend to get criticised and identified by what they wear whereas men get off scott free. It is so sexist. You wonder if Malcolm contacted her first and then decided not to wear his John Travolta white suit because of a potential clash.

It has been commented that Malcolm's announcement about the Snowy is the long-awaited Snowy River Hydro II. Before that gets into production we have the upcoming sequel. 2014 Budget - The omnibus edition.

How many politicians will complain about a cut in penalty rates on a Sunday? Does Parliament sit on Sundays? Politicians aren't retail, restaurant, fast food and pharmacy workers and certainly their hospitality is the worst in Australia.

Bonus points to the first answer that includes breaking the law in it.

Abstain if you have a pecuniary interest and the topic of negative comes up for a vote in the chamber. I double dare!!!!

Turnbull successfully avoided the 30 pieces of silver adage, settling instead for a bag of gold. Multiculturalism works as no religion was offended or left out.

Malcolm should be asked to withdraw his remark about Shorten taking backhanders. The rule book has gone missing from the chamber. Someone took it when Tony Abbott became Opposition leader and it has never been found since. It is probably with other tomes such as 'Decorum and Etiquette' and 'In the Best Interests of the People'

Will there be changes to 18C that will allow majority Government owned corporate CEO's only to say what the government believes should be said? Dutton can't argue there is a lack of free speech and effectively deny someone having the right to speak. I am being hypercritical whereas he is being hypocritical.

What do you call a group of senators? Anything you like, because they all have their heads buried in the ground to avoid seeing common sense and reality.

What do you call a group of MHR's sitting in the chamber in the morning?

Lost.

What do you call a group of MHR's sitting in the chamber at Question Time?

I dunno. What is the word for a group of clowns?

Why do they have a division when it comes to a vote. Is that because the numbers don't add up on a piece of legislation?

Politicians with a pecuniary interest in something shouldn't be allowed to vote on legislation to do with that interest. If a vote

was called on removal of negative gearing how many then would be allowed to vote?

By definition an omnibus (a bus) cannot be derailed as it was never on track in the first place..... Simple logic really.

Multiculturalism is sometimes seen by some right-wing conservatives as multi-occultism.

Don't get the Michaela Cash and Malcolm Turnbull press conference. Two flags, two podiums and four microphones. What sort of rating does that get on the terror alert system? Should we be alert but not alarmed by what they are saying or alarmed?

18C is rearing its head again. Malcolm is preparing the way. By espousing the polite view about multiculturalism, he can then let his conservative hard liners loose with a reworked 18C to denigrate with impunity the people he is saying are equal. Clever, clever work Malcolm. You will appear a saint come what may.

Multiculturalism means that we welcome anyone from any country to our country........ if they can play cricket or help us get a medal at the Commonwealth or Olympic Games.

Is Malcolm a barrister or a barista? Both take something pretty plain and ordinary, fluff it up with a lot of hot air, while in doing so make a great show out of something pretty simple, then leave you with a cup far from full and charge you a fortune for it.

I am not sure what some politicians want with the 18C changes. Under parliamentary privilege they can say pretty much what they want about anybody. I can't believe that they really wish to extend that privilege to the general public because you never know what might be said about them.

18C - The magic number and letter combination you drag out to fill the deathly silence when you have no real policies to push either in the party room or in the chamber. The LNP is bereft of ideas, needs a distraction or has people in it who have nothing better to do or say. Perhaps it is just some people on the right

wishing to be noticed who wish to advance the cause for change? A lot of hot air that should be driving a wind turbine instead of clogging up the fetid unproductive air that exists in Parliament.

The omnibus bill has been split. It now is two mini buses. Hopefully it may be be split even more and each piece of legislation will be viewed on its own merits. Heartily sick of the horse trading that takes place. "If you vote for this, we might do that." Nothing more easily broken than a politician's promise.

Ah Australia - Harmony Day yesterday. Perfect the next?

The combined effect of changes to 18C, the childcare package and the asylum seekers on Nauru and Manus would allow the government to legally denigrate the asylum seekers' children who if transferred to Australia, would take up valuable child welfare monies? These asylum seekers wouldn't be able to work and thus child care wouldn't be an option. Cunning lot these LNP's.

With the cut in penalty rates will McCormack take a cut in his travel allowance? I don't think so. Those who make the rules.......

"Europe is having a serious terrorist attack every week. Australia is having a terror attack every three or four days," says Bob Katter! However, Australia is having an error attack every three or four days based on your use of fake figures

(Trump has error attacks every three or four minutes)

I can see why everyone complains about "Your ABC". I have just watched a program that had the potential of a comedy but turned into a tragic farce. So called humour wasn't apparent, delivery of lines was poor and surely the director should have intervened so that the main characters speaking parts could be clearly heard. The setting was pretty banal..... too much greenery. I recognised some faces and now I ask myself why someone would want to impersonate a politician especially when they don't do it well. The writing was awful. I certainly don't recommend that you catch it on Iview. I am going to avoid it if it turns into a series. There are

much more profound things to do with one's life such as watching paint dry and grass grow. **My recommendation is that you avoid the program Question Time. Surely Michelle Guthrie this is one thing that should be cut to help the ABC meet its new stringent budget.**

Rushing through to debate 18C is politically smart. A committee sitting for a few weeks will just keep it bubbling in the background. 18C and same sex marriage need to be resolved quickly so that clear air can be given to the budget. The continued renewing of debate on these two issues is choking the life out of this government. But that's political climate change for you. A poor policy for renewables just won't work.

The casualisation of the workforce applies to parliamentarians in a few different ways. Some are very casual about recording their expenditure and even turning up at times. Others become casualties of the power games that are played or because of their own greed and stupidity. Some are pretty casual about the way they spend taxpayers' money.

Seems Dutton is the Libs, "please make it go away" person. Same sex marriage, asylum seekers and Tony Abbott....

18C and marriage equality are the hot topics. Amazing! The government wants to sweep these under the carpet before the next election or at least "dead, bury and cremate" them. So they bring them out now. Have people put up and shut up and then they can get things done that will actually earn them some votes. It is all about votes and distractions. It has nothing to do with policy. Strategies are being put in place to enable them to win the next election. It's not how you play the game; it is whether you win or lose. And these people complain that some of our high-profile sporting stars are poor role models for the young people in the country!!!

Security needs to be beefed up at the Australian Grand Prix. If a terrorist wishes to take out as many politicians as he/she can in one go, then Canberra isn't the venue. the Grand Prix, The Melbourne Cup or the AFL Grand Final will each give you a full roll call of past and present politicians. The ones I feel sorry for are the special helpers who accompany the politicians to clean up any mess that the gravy train splashes on them.

It is not all Howard's fault at all. The Middle East was an unstable environment well before the last lot of colonisation. However, Howard was in charge when the decision to invade Iraq was made. He had poor knowledge and was proven to have made a poor decision which since has caused the escalation of terrorism throughout the world. Both Blair and Bush since have had the courage and decency to state that they got it wrong. We are still waiting on Howard's response.

We need to realise that Parliament House is merely a symbol of democracy. It is not really a place where things actually get done and decisions are made. That happens in the backrooms of union offices and in boardrooms across Australia. Are our politicians in danger?... Yes. Are the police officers who guard them and us and soldiers the politicians send overseas in more danger?... Absobloodylutely. Newton's law. For each action there is an equal and opposite reaction. Howard's decision to join Bush and Blair and invade Iraq sees us still reaping the consequences of that action. Instead of a call for more protection perhaps we need to have politicians who won't play games, will get the job done and we can trust to make the right decisions on our behalf.

If the cyclone had hit Manus Island or Nauru would those there be transferred to safety in Australia by naval vessels? Not by Canberra (HMAS) anyway which was found to be unable to even come to the rescue of Queenslanders

How come politicians have the option of TGIT (Thank God it's Thursday) rather than us poor plebs have TGIF. At least we have POET'S Day. (Piss off Early Tomorrow's Saturday) to ourselves.

If an opposition's role is to hold the government to account for its policies, then why does an opposition have to even detail its own. Turnbull is doing an Abbott and speaking more like a leader of an opposition than a leader of a government. Either that or perhaps he is not proud enough of and confident enough in his own policies.

Both Turnbull and Shorten had little difficulty acclimatising in North Queensland. Both are trying to handle disasters in Canberra and are in deep water with their own parties.

If Australia actually manufactured stuff anymore, trickle up economics would work. Normal people are given money to spend. manufacturers would then have to produce more and thus more people would be employed and the system would feed on itself. Nowadays that can't happen. Trickle-down economics doesn't work either because tax cuts and government handouts to businesses just get siphoned off to overseas manufacturing. It would be better if the government hung on to the money and bought back the farm.

All those CEO's yesterday. At least with the photo op we now can see who actually is running/ruining the country.

Does the line "low-paid workers being found in high-income households" mean that the maids, chauffeurs, nannies etc. employed by the well-to-do are being exploited?

If the truth is that there is a loss in actual buying power despite the Minister's promise that "No recipient of FTB will have a reduction in payments as a consequence of these reforms," then the same actual loss should be applied across the board to let's say, parliamentary allowances and entitlements.

If the Senate has to work overtime and sit on Friday, what penalty rates apply to senators? They may have to delay their 37 day long weekend break.

With all those CEO's in Canberra yesterday, I googled what the acronym CEO stood for and came up with 'Cheat Every One' or

'Cretin Extremely Overpaid'. But you can't believe everything you read on the internet.

Years ago, we had state run power companies. Then supposedly to make things more competitive we ceded the power of control of these companies to private enterprise. Now these privately owned power companies can charge what they like, refuse supply and influence what other types of power can be generated. They are the real power behind the throne.

Amazing that if a humble employee in either a private company or public service position decided to abuse the entitlements on offer, he/she would be summarily sacked and possibly facing fraud charges. MP's need only pay it back and avoid further scrutiny. Perhaps Bron couldn't afford the airfare to attend the expenses review?

Name calling. Playing to an audience. Petulance. Being pedantic. Obfuscation. All strategies that toddlers try but they eventually grow out of...... unless they become politicians.

Politicians get all the perks. Why can't normal Australians have the option of a no confidence motion far more often?

I am thinking of forming a political party called NOTA. It should garner a lot of votes especially if it is on the bottom of the ballot paper. Voters will scan through and select None of The Above.

All those people in North Queensland's tourist resorts that were hit by Cyclone Debbie will be so grateful for Malcolm's pep talk. If they have a job left to go to, they will be working flat chat for less pay on Sundays. Gotta love timing.

Will Trumps defeat on a few key issues by his own party see him take his bat and ball and millions and go home? Should we ask 'What would Malcolm do?'

Details are 'sketchy' about Peter Slipper's portrait. Are we going to have our day coloured by Steph's bad puns? Perhaps she has brushed up on some new ones or will just draw on her past examples.

Was it really a game of "Chinese whispers" regarding the extradition treaty? Did Malcolm just mishear political advice?

Cyclone Debbie strikes North Queensland. Cyclone Pauline strikes in Canberra.

Will George Brandis's posting be determined by which embassy can be reconfigured the easiest to accommodate bookshelves?

The call will come soon enough, "Bring back Abbott!" It will be like Jurassic Park. What seemed like a good idea had terrible consequences. Will Turnbull look at the latest poll and just see it as fake news?

April

- Ongoing floods in Northern NSW cause the deaths of nine people
- Malcolm Turnbull makes a controversial decision to scrap the 457 visa program which allowed cheap labour to be brought in from overseas
- Tensions in increase in Syria as US attacks an air base in retaliation for suspected use of chemical weapons

There should be more money in the budget for policies to reduce family violence. Little changes and just having an app on your phone is bloody useless.

Snake oil, used cars and federal government promises. Can you spot the difference in sales techniques? I can't.

How many planes, subs or ships not being bought will allow some paying back of debt?

It seems that so many people will automatically be employed because of the Treasurer's small business incentive. They will all be in an office stamping papers saying "small business incentive application denied."

Nationally important infrastructure projects such as road, rail and port improvements are supposed to go through Infrastructure Australia to validate their economic benefit. Why has this process on occasions been circumvented? As rail and light rail can readily move more freight and people quicker, more reliably and more economically, why has there been a major emphasis placed by the Coalition on road construction?

Asian governments who decided to play the human pinball game of turning back the asylum seeker boats that Australia initiated, have scrapped that policy due to the outcry about the inhumanity of it. Are the members of parliament unable to hear the similar outcry of those in their own electorates?

There has just been a massive recall of cars due to faulty workmanship and poor-quality control. Voters should be able to rescind their votes if what they opted for is substandard and is not what they were promised.

It has been the practice for successive governments over the years to blame their predecessors for everything even after they have been in office for a number of years. It would be a novel thing if the current government accepted responsibility for things that happen under their watch.

The Coalition promised structural reform for taxation and that reforms would be taken to the next election. Isn't going to happen. Self-interest and business lobbying take precedence

We send immigrants off and tell them where to go. I think it is to the "Far Queue!"

If we were in a war-torn place we would want to move. Just because we are lucky, we have become selfish.

I am missing the spin. Bring back the pollies. They talk about nothing and don't make me think about things.

What a great segue. We hear about the suffering in Afghanistan and how little is being done and then quickly focus on our own first world issues.

I like the way we bomb the hell out of a country and destroy their infrastructure all in the name of freedom. 3 cheers for us

With the Palmer United Party losing its Federal Parliamentary members through what has been deemed as autocratic rule; the party has gone the way of other small parties and become a spent political farce?

There is so much hot air being thrown around between the two parties in the House of Reps that climate change is happening on the floor of the House.

We have cut foreign aid so the burden is now on charities. So, let's give money to charity and claim tax deductions. That won't fix the budget but the money will go where we want it to.

We spend a fortune on potential terrorist threats but women are in more danger from domestic violence than terrorism so why don't we spend money in the most needed areas?

What is the difference between a child in detention on Nauru and royal family apart from a billion or so dollars? Why do we treat them differently?

Australia has cut foreign aid. We are closing our borders to asylum seekers fleeing wars that we have started. We are being lampooned by China and the US because our climate change approaches are laughable. What sort of Australia do we want? What sort of image do we wish to present to the world?

Is anything in a politician's private life "fair game" to be used by other politicians, the media and comedians?

Is there too much responsibility placed on celebrities, politicians, sport stars and people in the media spotlight to be perfect role models for the rest of society? People take some responsibility themselves for the way they choose to behave.

We are making an expensive outlay for non-guaranteed results. We're paying emitters not to pollute in the hope that the incentive will work. What is stopping emitters from gouging the system and corrupt practices being used? Bugger all safeguards and assessment protocols are in place.

How many Australians are killed by terrorists? Many more Australian women are killed by violent men. Which is the bigger problem?

Shouldn't countries just deport "political prisoners" if they can?

We should vaccinate against poverty. Antivaxxers watch out!

Not that long ago, Tony Abbott put in plans to tackle the ice problem at exactly the same time scientists are reporting that ice exists under the surface on Mars. Coincidence? Perhaps someone has told him about the poles/polls changing on Mars with global warming. We can but live in hope.

"What sort of reputation overseas does Australia want and what sort of reputation does it have? are we seen as:

punching above our weight politically;

merely a food bowl and mining resource;

caring about our own and not at all about refugees"

When the price of iron ore drops, revenue drops for the government. To balance the budget, the treasurer has the courage to attack those who need support but lacks the courage to take on those who don't. Is this a conversation he would prefer not to have or maybe just at another time?

May

- Australian federal budget includes an increase to the Medicare Levy to help fund the National Disability Insurance Scheme, a new levy on the Big Four banks, and an increase in university fees.
- U.S. President Donald Trump fires FBI Director James Comey. Former FBI Director Robert Mueller is appointed Special Counsel for the United States Department of Justice, taking over the investigation into Russian interference in the 2016 United States Presidential Election
- An Islamic terrorist bombing attack at an Ariana Grande concert in Manchester, England, kills 22 people and injures more than 500 others.
- Indigenous leaders from across the country reject a bid for recognition in the country's constitution, deciding instead to push for representative voice to parliament.

Has anyone looked at the Application form for a visa that an asylum has to fill in? Apart from the sheer ludicrousness of some of the questions, it is a labyrinth of legal and public service doublespeak that only a solicitor might understand. There should be a plain English version or plain whatever language version. When confronted with the form an asylum seeker without adequate support would read the first question as "Can you make head or tail of this form?" If they answer yes then an official will tell them they have lied and to try again. If they answer truthfully to the import of the first question, they will be sent to directly question 217 which is really a statement, "Pack your bags! You have been marked as 'Return to Sender'

Can we put politicians on performance pay contracts? Given the performance by many of them each question time they will be owing us money. Good way to reduce the deficit!

Perhaps Masterchef could have some new contestants as there appears to be a lot of people cooking the books but sadly no-one with a recipe to fix the burgeoning deficit.

"It is a basic human right to be able to go out in public spaces, to shop, to go to concerts, to do our business, to take our exercise," Mr Turnbull says. The asylum seekers in Manus are being denied their basic human rights or aren't deemed to be human.

Mr Turnbull says what happened is "especially vile, especially criminal, especially horrific," because it was aimed at teenagers. Was he talking about the rise in Uni fees??

Is the Galilee Basin anywhere near the sea of the same name? Seems the owners of the Adani-Carmichael can walk over one and sincerely believe they can walk all over the other along with public sentiment.

I think George Brandis should check his bookshelves to see just how often the word 'girt' is used. Apparently apart from our national anthem the only other reference is from a memo from Peter Dutton. "Manus and Nauru are not only girt by sea but by barbed wire and lack of compassion as well. Keep up the good work!!!"

You would think that the cyber security guys would have their faces pixelated wouldn't you?

"In 2014, we had approximately 19 terrorism investigations. By 2016, just two years later, that number had risen to 72 investigations," he said. This is not an exponential rise. You need more data. It could be a spike. At present, it is a straight line so mathematically challenged people should check facts first. Perhaps the AFP are just getting better at their job and uncovering more of what may have already been there. Perhaps Commissioner Colvin would be better not to be alarmed but a bit more learned.

Lies, damn lies and statistics. How easy are we the public duped by those we have elected to represent us? We actually employ these people and if they fall below par in their work performance shouldn't we be allowed to take them to Fair Work Australia and see if their constant lying, feathering of their own nests and failure to meet performance targets (election promises) warrants dismissal?

Trump has blasted Germany because Angela Merkel stood up to him. He does it by a midnight tweet and not to her face. So, we have a strong alliance with a bully led nation. Germany is looking further afield to India and China. Perhaps we should follow Germany's lead and look to countries we now have more in common with and wish to be seen as an ally of. If the US take on China, will we become the lickspittle to a bully?

Apparently, we must lower our company tax rate for Australia to be competitive. Currently a large number of multinational companies have structured themselves so that their effective tax rate is 0%. If we lower the rate does that mean we must start paying them to continue their pillaging?

So green energy is now to include something that greatly contributes to global warming. How does that work? Are there various shades of green? The clean coal idea must be the blackest green there can be out of the 50 shades of green Frydenberg wants.

All those well-educated people sitting in Parliament and so few have a degree of common sense.

June

- Former NSW Minister for Mineral and Forest Resources Ian Macdonald is sentenced to 10 years in prison for criminal misconduct, for having corruptly issued mining licences.
- The Australian government agrees to a compensation package of around $70 million plus costs for asylum-seekers held on Manus Island.
- Victoria Police announces that Cardinal George Pell has been charged with multiple counts of historical sexual assault offences.
- U.S. government announces its decision to withdraw from the Paris Climate Agreement
- An Islamist terror attack on London Bridge kills 8 people and injures 48 others
- ISIS and other radical groups make terrorist attacks for the first time in Iran leaving 17 civilians dead and 43 wounded.
- Snap general election leaves Theresa May clinging to power with a hung parliament
- A fire at Grenfell Tower in London, England, kills 72 people and injures more than 70 others

Trying to work out how Channel 10 going into administration is somehow all Labor's fault according to Mitch Fifield. Has he been reading ScoMo's and Dutton's playbook?

Peter Dutton is right; we have taken back control of our borders; but at what cost? We have broken the International Refugee convention. We have lost our once high moral standing in the world. We have dehumanised people and placed them in concentration like camps for indeterminate periods. We have had a government who hides the truth from us about the state of affairs. We have paid billions out to foreign governments and private companies with negligible accountability. We have had a massive lawsuit taken out against us for the inhumane treatment and had it settle out of court. We have had a government four years ago who said that they will fix the problem and it still isn't resolved. You may have broken the back of the people smugglers business, Mr Dutton, but the internment and treatment of refugees has been a heavy price to pay.

"I'm not interested in speculating about lack of success," Mr Turnbull says when asked what happened if the party room will not support changes to energy policy. In effect he is saying that success is determined by the party room adopting it. That may come back to haunt you, Malcolm.

Malcolm Turnbull says, "What Australia needs is wise leadership, not glib leadership."

He goes on: "I have provided decisive leadership." Anyone else notice he said we needed wise leadership but he only offers decisive leadership.

A confidential agreement really? Dutton has just spilled the beans on what the payout was. He says he can't comment and then proceeds to. How Trumpesque! Next, he will suggest we build a wall when we already have a moat!

Perhaps my maths is wrong but every person in Australia would have to handover $21,000 each to pay off the government's debt. With only 24 million or so people to service the half trillion dollar debt perhaps instead we should sell off some assets. I think the large building on surrounded by Parliament Drive in Canberra is serving little purpose and could be sold off. (I think the Chinese may have investments in some of the occupants already). Then if we cancel the subs and planes....

Turnbull's backbench are revolting!!! His frontbench aren't looking particularly attractive at the moment either.

Is there no ceiling on our burgeoning debt? Can the government after so long continue to blame the previous Labor governments? The

Turnbull government are fiscally incompetent but there is no budget emergency. "We will be in surplus in four years". Mañana! Hakuna Matata! To which the public's response is Oy vey!!!!!!

Would Malcolm be better off falling on his sword than being knifed in the back?

So where are the detainees going to end up? That is the most important question. They will have a small amount to regenerate a life after two or more years of purgatory. They won't be allowed to come here and so boost our economy, will they? Or now that they are relatively rich they may be able to buy their way in like so many others do.

Perhaps Malcolm Turnbull could advise the asylum seekers where to invest their money. The Cayman Islands might not be the asylum seekers favourite though. They are probably sick of "tropical paradise" locations.

Leadership speculation is a figment of a PM's agitation.

Now if Turnbull was Trump, he'd sack anyone who disagreed with him. But Turnbull is not a dictator. He is merely dictated to by the Far Right.

Josh Frydenberg said "There was an overwhelming view in the party room yesterday that business as usual is not an option." then proceeds to tell the press and the public to mind their own business.

Pollies have their midwinter early. They have shortened the number of days of sitting so they have advanced the shortest day of the year to match. Such power. Such omnipotence. Such farce.

Now is the midwinter of our discontent and the politicians are having a ball!

If we looked at the cabinet ministers in the Abbott/Turnbull governments how many would get a pass mark? Dutton, Hockey, Robb definitely not. Julie Bishop would be about the only one, wouldn't she?

Amazing how a small number of politicians will be able to hold the country to ransom. I am not talking about crossbench senators, but the far right of the Liberal and National parties. On the area that has "vexed governments for over a decade" perhaps Turnbull should challenge the far right on the floor of the house by putting up a sensible energy bill that Labor and the Greens would support. Let the far right stand up for what they believe in and see how good their numbers are. But that's not the way the Coalition works is it?

The government has the power to change the rules on superannuation whenever it likes. Too bad if you have made a long-term investment based on what were the rules at the time. The Coalition might be keen to get their hands on our money to stop their burgeoning debt. So, we must invest in things they like for without coal we would just have an "ition" running the country.

What sort of politicians do we have that would enshrine inequality and intolerance into law? They would consign people to poverty. They would incarcerate those who have committed no crime except for being different, and that is no crime at all. They would promote the economic divide between rich and poor and the divide between those who own homes and those that can't get into the market. Perhaps these privileged people should climb down from their self-erected pedestals and walk a mile in the shoes of others. Have humans always treated each other the same inhumane way in the past? If so, have we learned nothing from history?

I can just see workers going up to their bosses and demanding a higher wage. In a perfect world, employers would agree and not then cut hours or redefine the job role and readvertise the job thus sending another person to join the Centrelink queues. But it isn't a perfect world. There is no level playing field for workers and employers and there is always the spectre of a company outsourcing to companies overseas or moving their own location there. That's just the way the fortune cookie crumbles.

If we ban all overseas political donations where will that leave our politicians? They will have to get out on the hustings and meet and greet the electors to try to secure our votes. I know that is more democratic but can we please have the "do not call register" and "do not knock" signs altered to exclude this unwarranted and unacceptable obtrusive invasion by these people into our everyday lives.

Peter Dutton's new super Border Security, AFP and ASIO group might even expand into the Army, Navy and Air-force. Imagine that! The last time someone did that pre-Trump and Putin was back in the 30's in Germany and Italy.

If Turnbull is charging the Snowy Hydro, what amount is he charging? Is he trying to boost the economy of the Cayman Islands? No wonder our electricity prices are going up. We've handed over ownership to the private sector for just about everything and all we have ended up is a lot of hot air in Canberra with no wind turbine in sight to use it.

Tudge, Hunt and Sukkar need to think carefully about a full apology to the courts if only to save Malcolm Turnbull's bacon. If found guilty of contempt they could be disqualified from parliament and thus the precarious numbers both in the party room and on the floor could be catastrophic for Malcolm. They may think that they are refusing to apologise on principle but could bring down a government.

Part of the problem that all legislation has in our parliament is the "us vs them" mentality that accompanies it. If one side proposes, the other side opposes. There is no real negotiation. The proponents think that they have all the knowledge and refuse to take advice, or possibly change things, in a "like it or "lump it" approach. Why do we continue to elect stubborn stupid people to parliament?

Amazing how good Abraham Lincoln was. The Gettysburg address lasted less than three minutes but said so much. Our politicians refuse to admit that our country does need a

"Government of the people, by the people, for the people." Josh Frydenberg proved this so eloquently when he said, "we have to proceed carefully ... my colleagues come first"

Dutton is doing his best to handle the war on error. He won't admit that the mistreatment of asylum seekers on Manus and Nauru was a mistake. $90,000,000 is a mere drop in the ocean....... Oops, can't say that because that is an "on water" operation.

Josh Frydenberg must have so many splinters from the fence sitting he has been doing trying to straddle two sides of the argument over energy. Simon Birmingham hopefully has learnt from this and is wearing protective underwear today.

I hope that the walls of the Coalition party rooms are fireproof. Last week the incendiary device was energy. This week, education. Who knows what is on future agendas? Perhaps the Clean Energy Council will grant the Coalition funding for producing energy from all that heat generated.

Malcolm Turnbull is actually leading a minority government. He is facing two oppositions. One on the floor and the other in the party room. Let's see how good he is compared to Julia Gillard at getting legislation through this hung parliament.

Congrats Malcolm in securing the Gonski 2.0 deal. The hardest negotiations weren't with the opposition or the cross bench but in your own party room. That took a lot of initiative and Simon Birmingham looks like the real Can Do Mr Fixit Man and perhaps Sco Mo, Dutton and Pyne could learn a thing or two. That's if they didn't think they knew everything already.

Forget the state of origin please pollies, think of the state you are leaving most Australians in. No real wage growth, half a trillion dollars of debt, second rate NBN, poorly educated by world standards, continually criticised for poor response to refugee crises and a country run by people who are the laughing stock of their own country.

Imagine if Dutton, not Birmingham, was put in charge of getting Gonski 2.0 through parliament. (with apologies to Pink Floyd)

"They don't need no education.
They just need thought control.
Teach citizenship in the classroom
Add Education to my role."

Don't the Senate do overtime? Isn't that part of their award conditions or are they just casual workers (extremely casual) and have had their penalty rates cut? They aren't in the hospitality industry or the entertainment industry based on some of the things they say. Procedural argy bargy and filibustering seem to be a way of filling in time. No wonder so little is achieved in the few days a year that parliament sits.

One Nation is an oxymoron because its members want to divide a nation. They pit White Australians against Indigenous Australians, Asians and Muslims and now want to have segregation of children with disabilities out of mainstream education and probably society as well. Let's hope that with this oxymoron party, their arguments/propaganda is starved of oxygen and are seen by the rest of Australia as moronic.

Should our politicians undergo an English Test similar to what Dutton proposes for immigrants? Given Pauline Hanson's comments on people with disabilities, perhaps so.

I am concerned that Dutton's new English (University level) test will be soon applied to all those Australians returning from overseas. Still, if politicians continue to take junkets and overseas postings, many of them may be prevented from returning and that is not a bad thing.

July

- Media reports indicate illegal trading of Medicare patient details on the darknet. This cause the temporarily suspension of Medicare cards as use of proof of identification.
- Scott Ludlam resigns as a Greens Senator for Western Australia after discovering he holds dual citizenship with New Zealand, making him ineligible for elected office. This was to be the start of a string of resignations and challenges at the High Court over dual citizenship including the Deputy PM, Barnaby Joyce.
- Russia and China urge North Korea to halt its missile and nuclear programs

If our morality makes us human then the way some people treat others such as asylum seekers displays their inhumanity.

McCarthyism being dealt out of the Immigration Minister's Office.

If we try to remove all discrimination can we leave that against Collingwood supporters last.

Human Rights don't only belong to Australians yet we deny them to asylum seekers.

Be careful what you tweet or you may lose citizenship

We may have had Magna Carta but where is our Aussie Bill of Rights?

People born in Australia are granted citizenship merely by that fact alone (unless you are the child of an asylum seeker). The indigenous people were not granted the full rights that go with that until 1967. Will we get to the stage when a Minister of the Government can arbitrarily remove a natural born Australian's citizen's rights without due process of law?

By detaining refugees who have no papers in concentration type facilities are we actually making them "stateless". If so, doesn't that go against the UN Convention on Statelessness which we are a signature to?

The legislature and the justice system are supposed to be at arm's length. When a Minister is given powers to override the justice system there is something wrong. The terrorists are winning by forcing the government to make Australia a far less free place. Should we let Australians fighting overseas return and then expose them to the full process of Australian law or keep them out based on a Minster's whim?

Most people aren't belligerent, intolerant or have their noses in the trough. They aren't homophobic misogynists with superiority complexes who belittle others and make fun of them with cheap shots and facile arguments. They work hard, go out of their way to help someone in need, and treat people as they find them without vilifying them because of their race, colour or religious or political affiliation. Based on who sits in the House of Representatives, is that place wrongly named?

With cuts in ATO staff numbers, who is going to check on the multinationals?

Foreign Aid goes to countries who don't have people who can vote in Australian elections, is that why it is being cut?

If unemployment is rising and interest rates are declining. Isn't the fiscal outlook just a matter of turning the graphs upside down. Hell, I can do that job.

Keating brought in super rules because the government couldn't afford to pay pensions for everyone. Now people want both. Are they double dipping?

If marriage is a lease, some people are really penalised for breaking the lease!

If the laws are wrong don't blame those who follow the law. Blame the law makers for not making changes.

Why is paid parental leave referring only to women?

With unemployment escalating where are the jobs for both parents to work and make use of the childcare support?

August

- The United Nations criticises Australian laws stopping same-sex couples who married overseas from getting divorced.
- Civil proceedings begin in the Federal Court, alleging that the Commonwealth Bank has committed 53,700 breaches of money laundering and terrorism financing laws.
- The UN Security Council unanimously approves fresh sanctions on North Korean trade and investment
- A military operation targeting Rohingya Muslims in Myanmar deemed as ethnic cleansing by UN
- Hurricane Harvey strikes the United States causing catastrophic damage to the Houston mostly due to record-breaking floods. At least 108 deaths are recorded, and total damage reaches $125 billion.

I'd rather that they spent $122 million on fixing the NBN or on science or both like New Zealand. Congratulations must go to the New Zealand scientists for their work on the Irritable Vowel Syndrome and the problems they have with consonants. At least that's what I thought I heard. The lag time on our fibre to the node NBN plays havoc with videos on YouTube.

Can the $122 million be docked from politicians' wages because we are after all doing their work for them by having a plebiscite?

I have a feeling that the plebiscite will only have one box next to it. "Do you support marriage equality?" Tick for no. Cross for no. Leave blank for no.

Malcolm Turnbull described the SSM issue as not being front and centre on people's minds, but important enough to have a plebiscite on the decision. I certainly hope that the next time we are dragged into a war, we are also given a say, not just have a captain's call on it.

What does $122 million buy these days? Fifty houses in nice parts of Melbourne and Sydney, or a large chunk of the Great Barrier Reef according to business assessments of its worth, OR political expediency and calming of the ranks in the Coalition Party room. What would you spend it on?

"We're not going to shut down democracy and debate because people here or there say outrageous things or defamatory things. We have a robust democracy." So says Malcolm Turnbull. Perhaps he meant "demoncracy" given the hell and damnation aspersions by politicians in Question Time perhaps it isn't.

Why not have the plebiscite cover a range of things including:
***Politician wage rises**
***Politician perks**
***Politician superannuation arrangements**
I am sure that some feedback may be helpful but probably not be seen as binding either.

It seems that Malcolm has Trust issues. He can't trust his party room and the majority of Australians based on polls find him untrustworthy as well.

I think Australia should vote on a Canbrexit. Let's leave the politicians in Canberra and move on. Their usefulness has for too long been overestimated and over-exaggerated.

There were believed to be only two types of leaders. The "I know the way I will take you there." and the "Show me the way and I'll take you there." The former is the one we need the second is the one we usually get. But now we have a third..... It's Malcolm and he's in the middle (muddle). His leadership style is "I don't know the way and I need someone to take me there."

Right now, three and possibly four senators may owe money for taking wages under false pretences due to their dual citizenships. If we can oust the rest of the Senate and all of the House of Reps, under section 44, we could almost afford a plebiscite.

24 hours in politics is said to be a long time. For Malcolm Roberts it may seem too short. I somehow think that 77 primary votes will not gain him another seat next election.

I find it strange that politicians are appealing to the High Court. The High Court has very wise and intelligent people on it. How could they find politicians anything but unappealing? The general public find politicians less appealing than used car sales people, real estate agents and lawyers.

The Coalition wants us to all have our two cents worth in the say over SSM. If my maths is correct, that's a long way short of the $122 million it is going to cost.

So, Trump is looking for a war to stamp some sort of legitimacy on his presidency. "All the way with Donald J" and our PM will take us to war with North Korea. Please have a plebiscite on the notion we should sacrifice our young men and women for an ignoble US President and his gun toting outlook.

I voted for someone to make decisions on my behalf and those elected get big bucks to do that. Those that want to renegotiate their contract should step aside and make way for someone who will have the courage and honesty to fulfill their contract

How many conservatives does it to change a light bulb? It seems just one or two in the party room to turn off the light on SSM. The others don't know how to do anything that will take us out of the Dark Ages.

The price of stamps must have gone up substantially. Fancy $122 million dollars worth of stamps for one letter to be sent by the government to each and every eligible voter and then returned. Can't understand why Auspost says they are losing money.

If a politician has dual citizenship does that make them two-faced?

Malcolm Turnbull, "You've been very naughty naughty children charging too much for electricity to consumers. Has someone seen my wet lettuce? They deserve a good thrashing."

The real question about the SSM debate is how soon Corey Bernardi will take to mention the word, "bestiality"

Barnaby thinks that if he pretends to be someone else such as Jack Benny, perhaps he might get away with it. The Jack Benny pose won't work. Poor Jack died and he was a US citizen. To quote the late Mr Benny, "I didn't deserve this award, but I have arthritis and I don't deserve that either."

"Barnaby rose in QT from his chair
As a man who shouldn't be there!
He shouldn't have been there many a day,
Oh how I wish he'd go away!"

Rank it is said has its privileges. When you look at those in the Senate who have opted to resign as the most fair and prudent thing to do, and the slightly fishy situation where a Minister and Deputy PM who are choose not to; it could be said, the ranker you are the more privileges you believe you have.

Ironic isn't it, but to change the section 44 rule on dual nationality, it can only be done through a referendum, not a plebiscite, postal survey or at the whim of the PM. But at least the result would be binding unlike what is likely to happen to SSM.

So many people supposed to be the elite minds of our country (in their words) fall at the first or 44th hurdle. You need to do your own due diligence. The law is the law. It may need changing but it was in place when they signed up to serve. The High Court needs to invoke the constitutional law for all equally. Clear the decks and start again with people who have a right, not just a self-professed right and privilege, to make decisions on behalf of the people they represent.

People in glass sheep farms shouldn't throw stones.... Barnaby those black things in the paddock are squishy and may look like

stones but they're really.............Oh McBarnaby.... you've done it again!

I am impressed that George Brandis has infinite mind reading skills. He knows how the High Court will rule on Barnaby already. Perhaps it is tarot cards, Ouija board or tea leaves. Check the meta data Georgie boy and see what will win the next Melbourne Cup so I can get a bet on early.

Being born in Tasmania can at times make you ineligible simply because the mainland MP's and PM's forget you exist. It is a wonder Peter Dutton hasn't thought of excising Tassie from the Mainland (as the AFL has done) and set up an operation at Port Arthur.

For a guvernmunt who prefusses to be the adults in the room, thur behaviour is su chuldish. (Written in Barnabese for ease of his understanding)

The SSM survey will be non-binding, so I wonder whether my local MP, Liberal Russell Broadbent, will take any notice of it. I don't know how he voted in the party room, but due to party room solidarity he must share some of the blame for the expense. If McMillan electors as a majority vote one particular way, will he just ignore it and vote the other? Does it depend on how the whole nation votes? McMillan electors elected him to make decisions on our behalf not to merely appease more vocal members of his own party. I am encouraging everyone in McMillan to take part in this survey whichever cause they support. At least that way we will find out what credence our local MP puts on the wishes of his electorate.

Can we please have the leather jacket clad Malcolm Turnbull back and get rid of the impersonator who has been stitched up in a conservative strait-jacket?

How many times do you think Malcolm has thought that the bunch of misfits and incompetents in his party would never cut it in the real business world that they hold sacred. He sadly stepped in at a time when the country was about to purge such people from

being in Parliament. He would have risen, admittedly as opposition leader, from the ashes and created a functional party that he could lead instead of being beholden to. Why did he not wait?

The knower of everything, also known as the supreme being has just looked at the Australian Constitution and the insane happenings caused by section 44. He waddles towards the edge of the abyss, his elongated ears rustling in the breeze and his last words echoed as he leapt. "Stuffed it up have I"

This saga has taken on Game of Thrones proportions in longevity and twists and turns anyway. All those people sitting around parliament making noises and actually achieving nothing. Perhaps we are watching Game of Drones.

Former defence minister and Tony Abbott ally Kevin Andrews used a television interview on Monday to assert "the best environment for raising children" was a family with a mother and a father. He did not quote what research but said "Overwhelmingly, the social science research points to that being [optimal]. Children brought up in those circumstances, as a cohort, are better off than those who are not."

This is the standard of debate that our pollies have started off the SSM marriage. The raising of families is not even part of the question being asked. Bring on the misinformation laws asap please Malcolm.

There are a number of MP's who are seeking a wage rise...... the remuneration tribunal are wondering why thirty pieces of silver are being sought.

Forget the missile shield, just harness Julie Bishop's death stare and Australia will be safe from foreign invaders unless they are British, Italian, Canadian or Kiwi of course.

Julie Bishop's diplomacy is almost Trump like. She has picked on the smallest ANZUS signatory and if they elect a Labor government, she says she would find it hard to work with them. Is she trying to influence another nation's election result? Something has rattled her cage because she is normally so calm and collected

and on top of her portfolio. I'd rather she stood up to the US than New Zealand. The issues are far bigger and more important.

If Joyce stands down, he loses his seat. Then he must stand again to be able to sit in parliament. Once back in he can stand for leader of the Nats and become Deputy PM and gain a seat in Cabinet. With all this standing down, standing again and sitting, will his knees take the punishment?

If the Kiwis really want Barnaby, then let us do a refugee type swap. They get Barnaby and we get the Bledisloe Cup.

Major train crash in Egypt. White supremacist rally in the US. Kim Jong Un and Donald Trump playing Russian roulette with nuclear weapons and here in Australia our Deputy PM maybe a Kiwi. Perspective perhaps but while the world goes to hell in a handbag, our politicians remain so fixated on themselves.

Can just see the next Four Corners investigation around New Zealand using Australia as a toxic waste dump.

Bob is putting the Katter amongst the pigeons!

So where is the SSM postal survey on the political agenda. Plummeting down I fear. LGBTI people are supposed to follow the law and refrain for the moment of calling themselves legally married. Politicians on the other hand seem to consider themselves to be above the law when it comes to their own predicaments. Self-sacrifice for them rarely gets out of the starting barriers. To quote Jack Lang, "In the race of life, always back self-interest; at least you know it's trying."

We should have already known about Barnaby simply because of all that "carping" on in previous years. Carp is an introduced overseas pest as well as well as being an anagram of crap.

Dual loyalties do need to come under heavy scrutiny and investigation. If you look at the party structure and allegiance to party room decision making, then you will notice that loyalties

are divided between party and electorate with the party having the greater almost whole share.

Can't believe NZ are claiming Barnaby. They have eradicated a lot of pests and diseases over the years especially foot in mouth. Barnaby has that as part of his DNA,

Just an interesting sideline to the preoccupation that our politicians have with themselves. The country seems to be running quite well with the politicians doing nothing except navel gazing. Do we really need them? Are they as important as they think they are?

There is a simple solution to the Barnaby crisis...... invade New Zealand! It may seem underhanded (or underarmed) to do so but it is a good and perhaps the only way to solve an even greater issue at the same time; that issue is getting the Bledisloe Cup back in our hands.

I think Barnaby has poorly enunciated the word. The whole thing is "hyper-pathetical" Next time people get knocked back at Centrelink simply because they have forgotten to cross a t or dot an i, I hope they use the Barnaby defence,

Tony Abbott is suggesting that the HC "solve this mess by sensibly reinterpreting the constitution in light of modern realities"

No, Tony. They need to rule according to the law. If the constitution needs changing to make it better match modern realities, it can only be done by referendum. So glad we have a separation of powers in this country.

Just Googled "liberal". One definition is: A liberal is someone on the left wing of politics — the opposite of a conservative. Also, a liberal attitude toward anything means more tolerance for change. Perhaps the Liberal Party needs to change its name.

Some may question they legitimacy of members in Parliament. Don Chipp wanted to keep the bastards honest. Perhaps he was also just questioning their legitimacy.

Spoiler alert…. The latest Game of Thrones has two illegitimate people heading off to battle. Maybe being illegitimate (in terms of being able to remain in Parliament) may be a badge worth wearing for many politicians. Some will wear it with honour (Ludlam and Waters) and some are unable to do the honourable thing.

When Big Brother flexes its muscle, town councils beware. The City of Yarra was within its rights to change what it does on January 26th. It opted to not hold a citizenship ceremony on that day. So now it is being punished by not being able to hold any at all. One would have thought that with all the issue regarding citizenship in the House, the LNP would want as many people as possible to become citizens.

I think that politicians should renounce their party. Their loyalty is divided. They choose their party over their electorate.

Perhaps Malcolm and George in the houses should butt out as well as they have already told us what the HC will decide.

Sitting in the gallery in parliament may not be suitable for those with a nut allergy.

Can we have a death stare off between Julie and Pauline please? Surely a betting agency will give odds.

The Trump administration has listed Pauline Hanson's One Nation Party as a threat to religious freedom in a new report released in Washington…… and wasn't it Trump himself who took so much time to finally getting around to condemning white supremacists and Neo Nazis for the Charlottesville tragedy. Now that puts a real (not fake news) slant on One Nation….. according to them worse than white supremacists and Neo Nazis. Give me Pauline over Donald J any day.

Good to see the LNP coalition people have all brought their 'so happy to be here' faces…… these will be photoshopped in later.

The house seems to be overcrowded…. but it's time for "Stripping back the coats of lies and deception" because "There's

a battle ahead, many battles are lost" as Penny Wong remains "Smiling as the shit comes down

She can tell a man from what he has to say"

Off to the High Court go Barnaby Joyce and Malcolm Roberts. Now there is a marriage of two minds made in heaven. Of course, in Australia that sort of marriage would not be legal.

I still can't fathom how New Zealand felt any compunction to claim Barnaby as one of their own. Heaven knows that many of us Australians don't want to claim him as ours when he opens his mouth sometimes.

There should be a simple form to fill in when applying to be a member of parliament. It should have one question only on it. "Are you a fit and proper person to make decisions on behalf of the people you represent?" the trouble with that approach is that almost all current politicians would have to resign.

"One would have thought simple honesty would have led her to disclose this fact to the Senate but she did not, she remained mute," says Senator Brandis. I would have thought simple honesty would have been for Malcolm Roberts, Senator Canavan and Barnaby Joyce to have said 'mea culpa' and resigned. Scott Ludlam and Larissa Waters set the perfect example.

There are aliens among us... they look like us, sound like us but aren't us. Like most B Grade science fiction movies of the fifties that people saw as real horror flicks, will we just see this tawdry affair in years to come as more a comedy than a horror drama, one that is lacking in any special effect and with poorly scripted bad acting?

Is finding out the truth a conspiracy? I would have thought that knowing the truth and concealing it would be more conspiratorial, but then I don't live in Julie Bishop's bizarro world.

There is so much blood letting in the parliament that the inhabitants are looking like zombies...... but how are we to tell the difference?

And if Pauline had sat down and no-one paid her any attention that would have been equally effective. She seeks and thrives on controversy and got a huge audience today. Brandis took the high moral ground and handled himself extremely well earning the plaudits of colleagues on all sides of the chamber. Pauline showed that you can wear what you like and her argument is that you shouldn't be able to wear what you like. Not clever really.

Abbott is right behind the PM now. He will support him to the hilt!

Smart move by Morrison. He will use the ploy of waving the guilt card at anyone who doesn't support the rise in the Medicare Levy. Great distraction from the fact that he and Joe Hockey didn't properly budget for the NDIS in the first place. On a wing and a prayer, he might just fool everyone.

Scott Morrison has the answers for everything. Just when electricity prices are soaring, housing affordability has dropped remarkably, wage growth has halted, banks are making squillions, he decides to raise the Medicare levy albeit for a worthy cause. The biggest impact will be on the most marginalised Australians who can least afford it but I suppose it is a case of "let them eat cake". Low income people would gladly give if somehow Scott could give them a magic pudding rather than a hologram cake.

Russell Broadbent should put up a private members bill to bring those people off the island. But sadly, private members' bills rarely get up because either side of politics gang up and preclude them from even making the agenda. Russell Broadbent can't even threaten to cross the floor on this one. There is nowhere to go to. He could do a Bernardi and sit in the crossbench. Perhaps if something of principle is that important, politicians should opt for that course.

Remember the Oath of Allegiance we were indoctrinated in when at primary school? "I love God and my country, I honour the flag, serve the Queen and cheerfully obey my parents, teachers and the laws." How inappropriate that seems now. But then again it was only a rote learned oath, not a declaration that you satisfied the criteria for election as a member of parliament.

The Golden Gumboot! Or as Barnaby calls it The Guldin Gumbutt or if he has a cold Dudded Dumbutt. No wait, the latter is what we call him.

Why is the seating arranged in a horseshoe shape in parliament?

So that there are no naughty corners. All those who are naughty are sent from the room. Strange though that some who probably shouldn't be there are allowed to stay. That situation is unasseptable. Make the Supernanny the new speaker!

So, what wine goes best with oysters? Don't ask Matthew Guy for his recommendation.

Treasurer Scott Morrison is encouraging older Australians to downsize and "free up homes for larger families". Perhaps he could ask all of his colleagues to come to the party as well and sell theirs off. Better still alter the capital gains tax and negative gearing rorts and free up the market. However, that may not serve the self-interest of the same colleagues.

September

- Australia and Timor-Leste end their maritime boundary dispute in the Timor Sea
- Unseasonably warm weather and strong winds see bushfires break out across New South Wales
- Russian President Vladimir Putin expels 755 diplomats in response to United States sanctions.
- North Korea conducts its sixth and most powerful nuclear test
- The Caribbean and United States are struck by Hurricane Irma causing at least 146 deaths and $64.2 billion in damage
- An earthquake strikes central Mexico, killing more than 350, leaving up to 6,000 injuredand thousands more homeless
- Hurricane Maria strikes the Caribbean hitting Dominica and Puerto Rico and causing at least 3,000 deaths and damages estimated in excess of $91.6 billion.

It is amazing that politicians seem incapable or unwilling to fill in forms properly and check personal details. If I did that in Centrelink it would be a case of "No soup for you today" (apologies to Seinfeld). These are people who make our laws yet are unable to follow them or choose not to. Heaven forbid that they should not be held properly accountable in the High Court. "The dog ate my renunciation of citizenship" is not a valid excuse.

Let the politicians pay for the electricity that they use in Parliament and then see if they wish to do something about pricing structure, or heaven forbid, renewables. Perhaps solar panels could be fixed to that horrible looking security fence or a wind turbine that spins with all that fetid hot air that emanates from the mouths of politicians, may reduce the costs of energy in Parliament House.

Joyce voted to keep himself in. Should he have stood aside for that vote? One wonders just how many of the pollies have ethics.

So much navel gazing by these politicians. Meanwhile the US fleet are heading towards Korea for their own naval gazing.

Christopher Pyne looks like jumping ship to another electorate. There's a saying about rats and sinking ships but I can't remember how it goes.

If it is Equal Pay Day then perhaps everyone should be paid on what they actually contribute to the community. Firies, ambos, teachers and police amongst others such as nurses would get a huge pay rise and our pollies, well some of them need to learn how to queue properly in readiness for Centrelink.

Barnaby says he is being completely transparent but he forgets that we can see through him. Parliament House is really a glasshouse and he has been caught throwing stones.

If Tony is flying all over the country racking up frequent flyer points and $74,000 travel tab which we have to pick up, does he hold joint citizenship both of the Warringah electorate and Qantas? Should he be sent to the High Court?

Senator Cash says getting more women into work is the key to closing the gap. So let's look at the affirmative action plan for the Coalition.... oh there isn't one. How many women in Cabinet? How many women on the backbench? Yeah that's parity at its best.

Australians must always find someone to hate. For years and it still continues, it was the indigenous people. New Australians post-World War Two became targeted. Then it was the Asians turn and now it is Muslims. The LGBTIQ community have done it tough for so long and right now are copping it worse than ever. Whilst I feel sorry for Lyle Shelton and his feeling of persecution, sometimes what you sow you reap.

ScoMo and Matthias are putting the fear of 'reds under the bed' into the economic political agenda. With all the bluster and

hopefully bluff that Trump and Kim Jong-un are using, it is almost ironic that the prevention of a nuclear holocaust may be only aided by both China and Russia working out a compromise.

I don't think that I want to watch North Korea's version of "The Big Bang Theory'

Regarding Turnbull's helicopter flight on the weekend, was he searching for a bounce in the polls? Maybe he was marking out a possible secessionist line where Canexit will occur. Let's hope it was the latter. The former is more lost than Leichardt ever was and the idea of Canexit, where Canberra secedes from the rest of Australia, would be a noble thing that many Australians would honour Turnbull with a statue that would never be defaced.

Peter Dutton wants to stop people trafficking, perhaps he should look at what he is doing to the asylum seekers supposedly under his care and protection. He sends them off to Nauru and Manus to inhospitable conditions at best. They are indefinitely detained. They become victims of violence, rape and mental health issues. Reluctantly and belatedly they are transferred to Australia for support and now they are to be transported back to the islands where their problems arose; to camps that are now closing. He is transporting these people based on an ideology that many Australians think is cruel and inhumane. Companies are profiting from his policy and that smacks of trafficking. His Ministry has expanded and has a bigger budget and that too sounds like trafficking. They could become indentured workers in Nauru and Papua New Guinea unless they go home to war torn countries. Dutton calls lawyers fighting such inhumanity un-Australian! If being Australian is supporting such barbaric practices, I may renounce my own citizenship.

So, the Liberals in WA want to Waxit. It will be a close shave though to get it through.

There is one house that is falling in value in Australia and it happens to be on the top of Capital Hill in Canberra.

Spiralling energy bills, rising rent, inability to break into the housing market, profligate spending by politicians who are out of touch with the real world, flat wages growth, full time employment opportunities dropping; in the tone of Dr Phil, "So how is trickle-down economics working for you?"

That security fence they have put around Parliament House in Canberra isn't working. Apparently, there are people inside who shouldn't be there.

Vietnam was known as the television war and we were involved for nearly ten years. Iraq was similarly a TV war lasting around six years. War with North Korea will last a few milliseconds and we won't even see it on TV. The TV execs won't ironically interrupt Australian Survivor to tell us.

The ANZUS treaty could be invoked if the US is attacked. But what happens if the US attacks first? Will Turnbull be doing a Holt and say all the way with Donald J? I hope Malcolm has had swimming lessons.

Just wonder what the test on Australian "values" will entail.

Q1: In voting on something that concerns you, should you abstain? YES/NO

Q2: What is the meaning of dual citizenship?

a) having allegiance to two countries

b) being able to vote in two countries

c) irrelevant if you belong to the LNP

d) all of the above

Q3: What is a Collingwood fan?

a) a cooling apparatus

b) a toothless tattooed ignoramus that supports a team that most people hate

c) a cross between a magpie and a fantail

Q4: The most powerful member of the government is

a) Peter Cosgrove

b) **Malcolm Turnbull**

c) **Peter Dutton**

d) **Tony Abbott**

Q5: Xenophobia, please explain in twenty five one syllable words or less.

"We are taking real action" with energy bosses. I suppose using a wet lettuce is a form of action.

Will Turnbull be hanging on to or hanging up on every word of the "leader" of the free world?

Urgent and unforeseen is Malcolm's continuing dip in the polls. Hark back to when he took over from Abbott promising so much. Hamstrung by the right he's become the nowhere man - the man on the stairs who isn't there and who we wish would go away.

If we send enough politicians to Korea and the North Korean nuclear accident waiting to happen, happens they will get a first-hand experience as to why nuclear power should be off the agenda.

"Warm and constructive" conversation between Trump and Turnbull? More like alarmed and destructive.

Free market enterprise is what all the conservative side of politics is all about. In Victoria, electricity used to be a state-run monopoly and all Victorians benefited from it. It was sold off by the Liberal state government with the promise that the free market would reduce prices.... an empty promise. Now the energy companies want to get out of coal and suddenly the conservative opposition in Victoria are wanting to buy back coal fired power stations. Either the free market system doesn't work or the right is moving well to the left.

Malcolm Turnbull, the only person standing between Peter Dutton being Prime Minister at the moment. Stay healthy Malcolm please.

Liddell is being said about coal fire power stations today. With AGL's statement perhaps those plans have gone up in smoke.

What we wanted to happen was for the parliamentarians to do their job and to vote yes or no. now we will fork at $122 million and then they can ignore the results of the survey anyway. Your taxes at work.... but not your politicians.

John Howard gave us no say when he changed the Act so I suppose we should be grateful

So, will the High Court also back Malcolm Turnbull's assurances that all the senators and MP's have done nothing wrong in breaking the law as outlined in the constitution?

Obviously from Malcolm's comments in Question Time he didn't think that the High Court Challenge was unforeseen and unexpected.

On to some more important conspiracy theories. After both appearing on the ABC's Offsider's program, Australia's soccer and netball coaches have managed under-performing teams. The question must be asked as to when Malcolm Turnbull appeared on the same program.

With a few before the High Court the Greens are an endangered species

Think of all the disease that could have been passed on to these animals from our politicians - cowardice, avarice, lack of ethics, morality deficiency...... geez I hope the antvaxxers didn't get a look in for these animals.

I noticed that there were no asylum seekers from Manus Island or Nauru at parliament for the Threatened Species Day. I suppose the $70 million to buy their silence included not turning up.

How many photo ops must our politicians partake in? Haven't they got something better to do? Oh, I see, they have but don't have the capacity to do it.

Kim Jong Un and Donald Trump may make Australians the most threatened of all species if Malcolm Turnbull doesn't decide to show them that we are an independent nation.

How many policies that have been taken to the last election have been watered down, been put on the backburner or been summarily dismissed? There should be some sort of warranty on such things and the public should be recompensed for false advertising.

I am sick of the horse-trading and politicking that goes on. A piece of legislation should be voted on. It is either voted for because the person elected thinks it is right or it is knocked down because it is wrong. Playing the game of "If you do this, I'll do that." is a poor way to get things done. Ethics and morals get thrown out the window as different barrows that are being pushed collide. we expect our politicians to do the right thing on behalf of their electorate, not on behalf of themselves and not on behalf of an ideology that someone else tells them they have to follow.

$122 million is being spent on the postal vote. If the High Court quashes the idea then perhaps, we can go to the High Court and challenge the expenditure on wages and perks our politicians get. They were unforeseen and unexpected expenses. Our argument would be that we thought that they could actually do something and would get something done.

If the High Court rules that the postal vote is out of order, then hopefully the vilification of, and lies about, LGBTIQ people will have a respite like you get in the eye of a hurricane/cyclone. Look at what damage those weather events cause and how they are becoming more violent.

Apparently, there was some consideration after the ABS computer glitches during the census to having McDonalds handle the SSM survey. Instead of "Do you what fries with that", people were to be asked did they want to allow Same Sex Marriage with that. However it was considered that some people would do the drive thru too many times during the survey period, and that may skew the survey results. i.e. weigh them down one way or another!

I am sure that Canberra is regarded as a remote location. Not only are the politicians remote from normality, they seem to be from another planet.

So many egos in the one room, so little talent. How did the pre-selectors get it so wrong?

It has been said that Question Time is just the theatre of politics. If it was theatre, this comic farce would have started off Broadway and closed after opening night. Audience members would have walked out after the first act. The script writer would have been pilloried and the actors would be back at Centrelink on a permanent basis.

If that's what passes for wit in Parliament then so be it. I had most of them pegged as witless trough feeders.

No point in Barnaby rising to answer a question because he has no answers, although he has a lot to answer for.

Question Time should be renamed Wasta Time

In the words of Elmer Fudd, "Shhh. Be vewy vewy quiet, I'm hunting Barnabies"

Worst floods in Bangladesh in 100 years affecting 100 million people and all we hear about is Hurricane Irma which is affecting around 2 million people. Goes to show that all lives are not equal.

**In times of trouble economically and politically, countries will start a war or goad someone in to a war. The think tanks get together and decide on who they can beat. America has made some bad choices in the past. Late to enter the First World War. Late also in the Second World War. Korea ended up as a truce. Vietnam was a defeat. Afghanistan.... well that's still going. The first Iraq war led to the rise of Al Qaeda. The second Iraq war and ISIS popped up its head. Now it is looking at North Korea. We have blindly followed the US since the Second World War. We are slow at learning lessons. We should try to persuade them that New Zealand might be a more winnable opposition unless it is determined by rugby.

No coal. And with solar and wind unable to store the power they generate in battery storage adequately as yet; we will have to rely on gas. Just watch those gas shares go through the roof. Invest now!

So, the Coalition is taking on a new role as a broker of power plants. I wonder what its commission will be? Probably about minus 25% as it will have to provide subsidies and incentives for someone else to take over what AGL quite rightly says is not worth spending any more money on.

The Coalition took charge in 2013. When will they own up to things that they have been responsible for? Or is it always a case for politicians that "it never happened on my watch"? In life that would mean that you could always blame your parents..... (Matt Canavan does that too!) and then your parents could blame their parents and so on. Mea Culpa should be part of the oath of office for politicians.

Anyone find it ironic that Mathias is in charge of the postal survey? He seems so unsure about LGBTIQ anyway. After all he was the one who called Shorten out as being "a little girly-man"

According to Labor, the Coalition is pork barrelling their seats 138 to 1. I am in a Liberal won electorate, pork crackling is thin on the ground here but hopefully things will change. I just love the smell of bacon in the morning.

Just want to know how you can put emojis on the Same Sex marriage survey form?

If you swap LGBTIQ people to 'bringing Manus and Nauru asylum seekers to Australia', Alan Fels would be right twice. "Despite the fact the majority of Australians are supportive of LGBTIQ people, unfortunately unacceptable sentiments are being expressed around the debate."

With all the dramatic changes in the severity of weather events caused by climate change, we now have Typhoon Un and Hurricane Donald hell bent on increasing the extinction of the world's population at an even faster rate. North Korea and the US have Weapons of Mass Destruction and they are both presidents. Any space left on that Mars trip?

The National Mental Health Commission, no less, is worried. Seems Matt Canavan has the age-old answer that has been debunked so many times, "grow up and get a spine". Forget Beyond Blue, his suggestion is beyond the pale.

Politicians wonder why we don't love them. Well I, for one, am extremely disappointed in the way they shed their morals and ethics like ill-fitting garments with the horse-trading and politicking that goes on. Like emperors without clothes, they cast off their remaining dignity and principles and are left standing in public naked to the world and so we see them for what they are. It is not a pretty sight.

Mr Joyce says when asked if the Coalition will have a Clean Energy Target.

"We will do the responsible thing."

But one wonders if they will accept responsibility for what they do and have done in the past four years.

I want to know whether these Senators and MP's who may not be eligible would be willing to give away their AFL and NRL Grand Final tickets they get as part of their "research". I for one would be happy to take them, at the price they paid for them of course.

According to Abbott it has been years "since gay people have been discriminated against, and just about everyone old enough to remember that time is invariably embarrassed at the intolerance that was once common", Nowadays we are more subtle apparently. We don't give them the same rights as others.

Tony Abbott who venerates Oxford should look at the Oxford Dictionary about marriage. Report from 2013 -"The Oxford Dictionary Is Changing the Definition Of 'Marriage' To Include Gay Couples. ... The new definition will include both heterosexual and homosexual couples to reflect the changing times".

Fizzy Beer or should I say Busy Fear. The shortened version of silver spoon socialism is called a spoonerism.

QT for Bob. He proves once again the old saying, "As mad as a Katter."

Barnaby able to answer a question without being shouted down by the Opposition. He seems flushed with success.

A win for Tony but a loss for the rest of Australia. No clean energy target. What dirt does he have on you Malcolm?

Be still my beating heart - question time - now only 20 minutes away. Watching paint drying or grass growing is a better way of seeing something actually being achieved, and it's far more entertaining.

The architect Romaldo "Aldo" Giurgola who designed Parliament House died just over a year ago. Luckily, he never got to see the vandalism that the new fence has wrought on his design. He would be rolling in his grave if he knew. We on the other hand can't even roll on the grass anymore.

Climate change is about the triggering of more severe weather changes. Hurricanes and Typhoons will become more violent such as the that hit Hong Kong and the US. There will be more severe floods e.g. Bangladesh. More snow for some places and more droughts for others. I hope the sand isn't too warm for your head where it is buried.

Let's look at Olivia Newton-John's song choices for her visit

Let's Get Physical - (while shirtfronting Tony Abbott)

Hopeless Devoted to You - (decrying political ideologies)

Summer Nights - (blackouts this summer caused by no energy emission scheme)

and finishing with Send in the Clowns - (addressing all MP's and Senators)

"There's no such thing as a minor child sex offence," Mr Keenan said. Caveat to be added..... unless you are a priest.

Ironic isn't it that "Somewhere Over the Rainbow" is a song about Oz and we here in in Oz fear the Rainbow Connection that SSM marriage might bring. If only courage, knowledge and a heart were to be found in our politicians then the vote would be passed without the waste of $122 million.

As a follow up to Threatened Species Day we get a fence around Parliament House???? Politicians obviously didn't follow Matt Canavan's advice to 'get a spine'.

Apparently, they are changing the signs as you are entering Canberra. They now will read, "Welcome to La La Land."

They should paint the fence with the same material that the Coalition used to write their energy policy. That way no-one would see it.

This new Parliament House fence has been sponsored by???? My guess is Donald Trump as a trial for his wall across the Mexican border.

Can we get Scott Morrison to cast the forcefield spell "Protego Maxima. Fianto Duri. Repello Inimicum." around Parliament House like the professors did around Hogwarts? That way the ghastly fence could be removed.

To whomever decreed that we needed such a hideous addition to the beautiful grounds of parliament House, "Bollards to you!!!!"

Will that new security fence keep dual citizen MP's and senators out? If not, why then is it being built?

Will Morrison take up the challenge and up the stakes on who is trendier by mentioning something about the Kardashians today?

Should the people at the AGL/Government meeting have been drug tested as they certainly heard different things.

Suggest that you look at the one question we are being asked and you will find that it is just about same Sex Marriage. People will conflate that with other ideas. The Parliamentary Marriage Amendment (Marriage Equality) Bill 2015 was a private bill that never got up.

Regarding the contradictions between Frydenberg, Turnbull and Vesey, I think each heard what they wanted to hear at the meeting. I'd plumb for Vesey though as he informed the Stock exchange and thus put his directorship on the line. Frydenberg and Turnbull have less to lose as politicians are known for their lack of understanding of the word truth. I assume no recordings were made nor minutes taken. If they were under the secret police state that has become Canberra, we may know in about thirty years. And it won't matter as by then as all three will be dead or in their dotage and Liddell will have closed in 2022 anyway.

I'm glad the question in the survey is fully written out. I am sure that a simple printing error may have occurred by using the acronym SSM. A simple slip and it becomes S&M.

How many solar panels will fit on the Liddell site? Maybe wind turbines too. A joint AGL and Elon Musk revamp maybe?

Craig Kelly has accused AGL of speaking with a "forked tongue". He has called AGL "probably one our biggest corporate villains". I am sure that his copy of 'How to Win Friends and Influence People' is still in pristine condition.

If AGL is a business and the Coalition believe in free market enterprise, then why won't it let AGL do the right thing by its shareholders? Perhaps Malcolm should do a Victor Kiam and like AGL so much he buys the company.

Got rung up by Ipsos and asked to do a survey. Was strange as I thought my number was silent. The surveyor seemed most affronted when I said I wasn't interested in doing the survey. He tried to make me feel that I had to answer the questions and was

being treasonous not to. I chose not to participate as I was concerned that somehow the call was being recorded and end up in Brandis's metadata collection. How many bookshelves does he need to get to house all that?

You wonder how any Minister gets anything done when they have to research for one liners all the time and have to have their voice heard non-stop to support the party line...... oh that's right, not many of them get much done.

So AGL wants 90 days before they cut off the power. Some electricity providers give their customers less if they can't afford the exorbitant power bills. So from Turnbull's point of view it is a win. 90 days brings it just before Christmas which is not Parliamentary sitting time so it will be lost in the news cycle and non-ratings period. Another smart move Malcolm. You are proving quite agile.

What happened yesterday in Parliament? As usual nothing of significance that will change things for ordinary everyday Australians. It would be wonderful and a complete shock if these politicians actually did something that was worthy of the money, they get paid and was of long-lasting benefit to Australians.

Politics is the thing that hamstrings the governance of a country.

With all those supercoach and fantasy team games out there at the moment, here's my best guess for a government team from the players in parliament.

PM - Penny Wong
Foreign Minister - Julie Bishop
Education Minister - Simon Birmingham
Attorney General - Mark Dreyfus
Treasurer - Chris Bowen
Infrastructure Minister and deputy PM - Anthony Albanese
Defence Minister - Marise Payne
Social Services Minister - Christian Porter

Health Minister - Catherine King
Finance Minister - Mathias Cormann
Climate Change, Energy, Environment Minister - Mark Butler
Immigration Minister - Richard Marles
Industry Innovation and Science –Scott Morrison
Employment Minister - Tanya Plibersek
Trade, Tourism and Investment Minister - Joel Fitzgibbon
Energy Minister - Josh Frydenberg
Indigenous affairs Minister - Nigel Scullion

These are my main ones but can't find a job for Turnbull, Pyne, Joyce, Burke, Shorten or Dutton. Happy to put them up for trade because they put politics ahead of ministerial duties.

There is a difference between the words normal and normalise. Whilst the percentage numbers of LGBTIQ people in the community are low, perhaps it is the right time to normalise them into mainstream society by giving them equal rights. A large number doesn't necessarily make things normal. Collingwood Football Club boasts that it has the largest supporter base and one can hardly call these people normal

"Why do some senators let others, let other people's value judgements push them around and control them?", Senator Roberts wants to know.

Oh, how those words will haunt him post High Court decision.

Pauline Hanson would like a referendum on marriage??? Referenda are used to change the constitution. Marriage isn't in the constitution so is she asking that it be put in there?

The issue we have with Liddell and Hazelwood is that they are tired outdated generators and the cost of maintenance, repairs and an upgrade makes them not economically viable. They won't get sold without a massive subsidy from the federal government. Anyone buying them would need to factor in that they are also going to have to pay for the clean-up costs when the plant is closed.

The Coalition may accuse Labor of doing people out of jobs but money would be better spent paying out workers with the leftover going to renewables and storage options, rather than on an enormous subsidy. It wasn't that long ago that the Coalition refused to subsidise a failing industry - the car one. They quite rightly said that it would be throwing good money after bad. Things change however when coal is involved.

What a shame that Penny Wong is in the Senate. If she was in the House of Reps, she would be a great replacement for the current leader of the Opposition. Imagine the outcry when a female, openly homosexual Prime Minister was elected. So many rednecks would not see that she would get the job hands down on merit.

Gay people are as socially responsible as heterosexuals. They are an extension of a family and many raise a family. They are members of the community who many people care about and who have rights just like everyone else. Currently they are being denied one basic right and that is what the debate is all about. Should they be extended the right to marry? That is all that people are being asked to express an opinion on. However, vilification of people on either side of the argument will soon incur a fine of up to $12,600 so we all need to be mindful of what we say.

Has anyone thought of pumping excess hot air from Parliament House to power a generator? That would solve all the future energy problems. I know that parliamentarians have huge breaks but I understand that the hot air lingers like broken promises.

One wonders whether Stuart Robert will tell his father to mind his own business.

Marriage is seen as both a right and a rite. For the LGBTIQ however they are allowed neither. Why are these two 'rights' seen to be so wrong?

Imagine if party politics was taken out of government? Would we get a better run country? Would there be more reasoned debate?

Would decisions be made quicker? Would electorates be better represented? Would we get a better calibre of people in parliament? Maybe it is worth a try? Couldn't be any worse than what is happening now.

John Howard had no qualms about changing the marriage act and moving on. Hypocrisy thy name is Howard.

Possible solution for the energy crisis could come from the fitness industry. Gyms seem to be open 24 hours a day. Think of all those treadmills and bikes that could be powering the country. In times of shortfall drop the price of membership. Could help with the health budget too.

October

- Toyota ceases vehicle production in Australia
- The High Court declares Barnaby Joyce, Fiona Nash and Malcolm Roberts were ineligible for election. Former Senators Larissa Waters and Scott Ludlam were also declared ineligible. The High Court declared Matt Canavan and Nick Xenophon eligible for election
- 58 people are killed and 851 injured in a mass shooting in Las Vegas
- A truck bombing in Mogadishu, Somalia kills at least 512 people and injures 316 others.

"Life is too short to.....
   a) spend it listening to politicians
   b) waste time thinking politicians aren't self-serving
   c) think politicians will get anything done
   d) all the above
Question Time being televised.... It's lights, camera, inaction.

Kim Beazley, the ultimate living proof that nice guys and politics don't mix.

In 2010 Malcolm Turnbull said "We have to make decisions today, bear costs today so that adverse consequences are avoided, dangerous consequences, many decades into the future." He said this in regard to climate change. The climate has changed for Malcolm. It is no longer expedient to do the right thing. He now lives for the day, eyes firmly fixed on the past, hoping like hell he has a future.

Not wishing to doubt Senator Hanson, but where is the scientific evidence that "the science isn't there"? Too much time with Malcolm Roberts and things rub off.

The security fence is almost like a wall as if Parliament House has seceded from Australia. And if those in it have, then why are we paying their salaries and our taxes for them to squander? There should be a Checkpoint Charlene and those who wish to leave should be vetted, perhaps in Peter Dutton style. Our own Border Force revenge.

That security fence around Parliament House is just ... well.... offensive!

How does Malcolm stop Tony being a back seat (bench) driver? Perhaps by showing just what he can do now that he is in the driving seat. Floor it Malcolm!

Tony Abbott's Christmas song, "All I Want For Christmas Is My Old Front Seat"

Tony Abbott is running the party.... or should that be ruining the party.

Amazing how a simple typo says so much. Sinister for Border Security, Peter Dutton ....how apt.

There is one power issue that the Liberals need to deal with. Just who is in power in the party?

Michael D. Higgins may be able to tell Malcolm how to successfully manage a same sex marriage legislation program. He might help Malcolm boost his poll results by showing him that there is indeed gold at the end of the rainbow.

So, this is supposed to be a free market yet subsidies are flying left right and centre. Renewables get some, coal gets some. Adani want a billion dollars in cheap loans. Let the market decide if you believe in free enterprise. Give them nothing just punish the polluters and see who comes out on top. A counter proposal is to nationalise the energy sector including mining and then the government can decide what to do with our resources. Yes, they are ours! At the moment the government is in no-person's land in between. And we are paying the price.... literally.

Abbott returning would be a zombie like performance. No CGI just a poorly scripted poorly acted horror film from the 1950's

Compare the wages growth graph with the opinion rating of the government. Both well below par and hardly moving. Strange that the government doesn't realise that the opinion polls graphs run inversely to housing and energy prices.

Mr Abbott demurred on the issue of polls saying, "I think the focus should not be on the polls. The focus should be on being the best possible government." And where can we get one of those? Been a long long time since we had one.

Just over a third of people want the government we have. Just over a third of people want the alternate government. That means that nearly two thirds of people are unhappy with the state of government or future government in Australia. I would have thought 50% approval would have been the bottom line for a pass mark. Government is not meeting acceptable levels of customer satisfaction and it is heavily in debt. Holden and Toyota were faring better when they closed down.

No washing machine ever made will be able to match the spin cycle that we will see after the announcement about what the government will be doing about the only recommendation yet to be accepted of the Finkel Report. Frydenberg will be hung out to dry!

An asylum seeker somewhere
Heard of a man who didn't care
Who said, "I won't let you in to stay
Piss off to the USA
Or go back home if you dare
Apart from that you're going nowhere
Cause my name's Peter Dutton
I alone say just who can come in
We may have boundless plains with which to share
About refugees I just don't care."

I am sure that Tony had a hand in the acronym NEG (short for Negative). He was probably just reliving a moment from his Opposition Leader days.

Turnbull, our wonderful Don Quixote and egged on by his own Sancho Panza, Abbott, are tilting at windmills, dreaming the impossible dream that they will succeed in defeating what they see as the injustice that renewables are the way of the future.

According to Malcolm, "I am confident common sense will prevail". But if he can't manage to get it in the party room, what hope has he got in the House?

My one real concern is whether GST will apply to the bottled air we will be soon forced to purchase.

Turnbull speaks of the art of compromise yet fails to realise that it has the word 'promise' in it. And those he continues to break.

Coal is a renewable energy. It just takes time.... a long time. A couple of Ice Ages, some catastrophic weather events, maybe an asteroid or two may speed up the process a little.

There will be a big boost for tourism from the energy policy. Already new posters are out saying "See the Great Barrier Reef before it becomes not so great." Several inland towns are also looking at population boosts as the seas come to meet them. A win for all!!!

The Pope recognises climate change and the need for renewable energy but a mere abbot controls what happens in Australia. Heresy!!!!

Our government is so busy horse-trading to get policies through that they have lost sight of the fact that swapping a Winx or Black Caviar for a nag bound for the glue factory isn't a great deal.

If I want the ear of the Prime Minister, I need to see a lobbyist. If I want other certain parts of his anatomy then I need to see the far right of the party as they have control of those.

Can we add a section in our Constitution such as 44 Part vi which would stipulate that politicians shall be incapable of being chosen or of sitting as a senator or a member of the House of Representatives if they are bloody incompetent?

The money for the security fence could have been better spent. Who would in their right mind attack our politicians? No-one is going to storm the barricades. Apathy is rife in Australia and our politicians lead by example.

While the world is undergoing major catastrophic weather events, Australian politicians have decided that underground sequestration might save them. Unfortunately, they are experimenting with just burying their heads in the sand. Or is it that they are searching for more fossil fuel and gas deposits?

"A crow is loudly making its presence felt in the background" Was it a Graham Kennedy Crow that was calling? Because that is what many Australians will be thinking.

It will be a "party" room this morning. They will be celebrating the success of the right wing and the probable demise of the Prime Minister that promised so much and delivered so little. Tony will get his old job back - leader of the opposition! So both sides of politics will be "partying" this morning. The only difference will be that the pinata in the Lib's party room will contain coal.

Adani billion dollar loan just needs to be ratified and everything will be hunky dory. Gotta love the Libs and their desire to relive the fifties.

Malcolm has gone to the Dark Side and the Farce is with him.
Malcolm "Clayton's" Turnbull - the Prime Minister you have when you are not having a Prime Minister.

If the government can ignore the expert advice of a panel they set up, what hope have we that it will heed the advice of a $122 million survey?

I am super impressed. What hold has Tony got over Malcolm? Was there a special deal done? Is there incriminating evidence that is being used to blackmail Malcolm. Like Luke Skywalker he has been asked to go to the dark side. But unlike Luke, there is no fight left in him. So, Malcolm maybe the farce is with you.

Climate change is all about the creating of extreme weather events. There is no climate change in the Liberal party room. The only extreme whether event is whether Tony will get his old job back.

So much for the notion of democracy where it is one person one vote. After the High Court ruling, we may have someone who received less than fifty votes ruling on legislation, perhaps with the balance of power. Our energy, defence, immigration policy etc. at the whim of someone who received such a poor response from her state. It beggars belief.

Watching Question Time on the ABC
"Horror movie right there on my TV,
Horror movie right there on my TV,
Horror movie right there on my TV,
Our pollies seem to be going insane."
(apologies to Skyhooks)

Will Malcolm get a bounce in the polls from this new energy policy? Personally, I think it will again be a NEG one.

Malcolm has acknowledged that politics is the art of compromise. He certainly is someone who has been compromised!

Malcolm, just a hint..... a bipartisanship on energy policy is one that usually has been worked on together and agreed to by those involved in its development. Yours has been developed by your party with no consultation except with your own right wing.

Malcolm complains about a power bill he has, but if he lived at Kirribilli or at the Lodge he would have no power bill. Still be power crazy but he'd have no bill. (except perhaps the opposition leader, Bill Shorten who may remove him from power next election.)

It's predictable. When a question is asked and you don't have the answer, you target the person........... same ploy used by both sides. Goes to prove that neither side has any answers.

I think that Sarah Hanson-Young is just checking whether Malcolm has booked in for Survivor. He may be cast out of the Liberal leadership when the tribe has spoken.

You will never guess who said this! "One of the key problems today is that politics is such a disgrace, good people don't go into government." Okay.... so, you knew it was Donald Trump. He reaffirms every day that he is not a good person.

For politicians who work part time and get paid full time plus allowances and a brilliant pension, they don't recognise that those who work part-time don't get paid full time wages.

Why are the state governments addicted to the revenue from gambling? The GST doesn't deliver enough!

Surely someone has got to ask the most important question of the day. "Now with Gary Ablett Jnr, joining Joel Selwood, Patrick Dangerfield and Mitch Duncan in the midfield at Geelong, who will be able to beat them? Will the ACCC investigate?"

So, Xenophon leaving will that be cast as a NEXIT move?

Is there a values test for politicians? If so, how many would fail? How many would need some very very deep soul searching to find where they left them? Would many have some in pristine unused condition? But then again, we elect them more often than not based on what they say, not the person they actually are. We don't set too much of a value on those who represent us, do we?

I understand that we are still awaiting on lifeboats to be delivered. They have been outsourced overseas and apparently Defence Department leaks are causing issues. The Defence Procurement Minister (Mr Fixer) has suggested that a hole be drilled in the bottom of them to let out what has leaked in, that way they will double as submarines.

Is Dutton still banging on about the citizenship test so that those facing the high court may be shipped overseas because they fail to pass the values test?

According to the NAPLAN robot Malcolm's test results read like this:

Stricter citizenship test – fail

No price set on emissions – fail

No-one left on Manus or Nauru – fail

Budget under control – fail

Appeasing the right-wing faction - marginal pass

Changing poll numbers to a positive - fail.

There has to be wins somewhere for Malcolm but none spring to mind except Gonski revamp and that was a Simon Birmingham victory.

A certain large company may need the massive tax cuts promised to pay off the fines imposed by Britain and the USA. Even with the generous Australian government handouts in the form of tax cuts, there may be nothing left to pay for any fines ASIC eventually get around to imposing.

Has Turnbull now called Tony's bluff? Frydenberg may be denying things regarding some sort of pricing on carbon, but it's there in the fine print and I'm sure that Tony will not like to see a carbon copy of what Labor had been suggesting all those years ago.

With Brandis's speech it seems the Liberal party's Xenophonobia may be over. Someone please explain that to Pauline.

The ABC may be an obvious place for cuts but the savings made would be minimal when compared to not buying as many planes and subs, not subsidising any form of energy, collecting tax from multinationals, still paying MP's who have lost their job lots of money in terms of perks, pensions and super before the rest of us can access our own. The ABC could save money by not telecasting Question Time. We also might get a better standard of debate if members knew that no-one was watching.

So, the legislation defeated in the Senate such as the Uni fees, Dutton's citizenship changes and others don't get a mention? I'm happy to acknowledge successes but you should provide some of the shortcomings as well just to provide a balanced perspective.

So, as the Seven ride off into the sunset after the High Court Judgement on Friday, will they be seen as the Magnificent Seven or the Insignificant Seven?

We won't be taking any Rohingya people who have had to flee Myanmar. They have now been branded stateless by Myanmar and Dutton's first action is to send them back to the country they came from. The ethnic cleansing which is a polite way of saying state sanctioned mass murder has evoked no response from Dutton. He really is the anti-immigration minister, isn't he? Bangladesh, one of the poorest of nations, has been left to do the heavy lifting while Australian politicians seem glad that those fleeing potential genocide are too weak to get on boats.

There was movement in Parliament, for the word had passed around

That the rep from Point Piper had got his way,
He had reNEGed the energy crisis - Left Tony trussed and bound,
But he'd have to watch his back if he chose to stay
He's taken on all his deriders from across the aisle and behind
And will overspend billions on the Snowy River 2,
But to balance it all up he'll help Adani build his mine,
Just shows this Man for Snowy River hasn't got a clue.
(apologies to Banjo P)

I may have missed something but has anyone raised the details of The Climate Council's 'Earlier, More Frequent, More Dangerous: Bushfires in New South Wales' report just released and the fact that mid spring Tassie has 70 ongoing bushfires burning already. Tony Abbott may pour cold water on these arguments but he'd be better off saving it as a volunteer firie in NSW to help put out these Climate Change induced fires this summer.

I would love to have the people who negotiate parliamentarians' EBA in my corner. Not only do our elected representatives get handsomely rewarded when employed including perks for many involving free meals accommodation and travel; when they lose their job they get to access their pension and superannuation well before mere mortals and some get an office and ongoing perks thrown in. If those negotiators aren't busy could they come and talk to Centrelink on my behalf.

Inspired by the madness of Canberra and to the tune of Our House by Madness

Pollies say they do their best
But they lie, or it's said in jest
They are pretending to care
Eyes open but sound asleep
It's enough to make you weep
At all of these clowns
Our house, surrounded by a fence
Our house, surrounded by a
Our house of which we're not proud
There's always nothing happening
Though it's usually quite loud
In cuckoo land above the clouds
Someone turn the volume down
Or get rid of these clowns
Our house, surrounded by a fence
Our house, surrounded by a
Our house, where nothing makes sense

If there are standing orders in parliament why do politicians care so much about losing their own seat?

Based on the standard of debate perhaps Question Time should have a suspension of standing orders every day or just be suspended entirely. An amendment for the constitution that would receive a huge positive vote would be the proroguing of Parliament for the period between elections.

Malcolm would rather he had more sycophants around him than people who have raided the cutlery drawer.

You have got to hand it to politicians. They are such method actors. They lie because they have convinced themselves that the lie is the truth. There is no pause, no slight intake of breath, no overt body language and I'm sure their heart rate doesn't change. Wow..... first class acting. Shame they are so bad at governing.

Michaelia's assurance to Turnbull has not cleared the muddied waters. It would have been better if she called in sick and there was no Cash for comments.

One sign of desperation in political battle is the playing of the man and not the ball. Looks like the Coalition dropped the ball on day one of its ascension to power.

Turnbull makes a good point. There is supposed to be a separation of powers. The politicians create the laws. The police investigate those who break the laws and the justice system try those brought before them. The word supposed has a meaning of "generally assumed or believed to be the case, but not necessarily so". 1930's Germany combined all three areas and even had the media thrown in for good measure. We are not at that stage yet but every day it looks a little closer. Dutton gave it a boost along and now Cash has helped out too.

Is Michaelia a tool of the far right? Can Turnbull steer her to middle ground? There may others trying to lead her to the dark side and proving Turnbull is still having difficulty with Cash converters

"Nearly time for some representative democracy in the people's house." too true we have been waiting since the turn of the century..... and I'm not saying which one!

On financial matters; don't you like how free market thinking works. Bunnings entry into the British and Irish markets appears to be a Masters stroke.

The raid by the AFP at the behest of the government shows that the Coalition really do see Shorten as a threat now and not the wimp that the public see. Just goes to show how scared they are of losing.

So, Kennan said it was Cash. Cash has gone 'wazzanme'. Teamwork at its finest. Maybe things just happen in Canberra and no-one knows!

George Brandis finally worked out what to do with metadata. Hand it over to Michaelia and see what she can make of it.

Yesterday the ABC and Labor were said to be in collusion. But by the end of the day the AFP and the Coalition could have said to have been the same. when will politicians realise that their job is to ensure these bodies work independently and are not at the beck and call or to be used as scapegoats by political bodies?

If we only had $122 million or so floating free it could be used to reduce mortgage stress on families. Oh wait... we did have ..... but politicians decided that they wouldn't do their job and it was frittered away on the SSM survey.

I wonder if a group of us got together and raised issues en masse about things we are dissatisfied with what the government is doing or not doing, we might have the AFP knocking on our door.

"In a neat trick of timing, the Registered Organisations Commission will appear before a Senate estimates committee early this evening." How on earth could someone believe that the police raids and damage to Get Up and AWU's public image is just a coincidence?

Linda Burney's tragic loss just reminds us that despite the way we may perceive politicians, they are very much human below that facade.

So, what is Get Up and what is so wrong with it? Is it a lobby group? A political party? Something that is illegal? Or maybe just

a group that raises objections to the way governments are running the country? As a political party or lobby group it would need to be registered. If it was an illegal group it should have charges laid against it. Otherwise it has the same rights as any other group such as the Australia Institute, Fabian Society etc. Why is it having its name blackened? Is this an overreach by a desperate vindictive government.

Sourdough would be any money paid by taxpayers for coal subsidies, wouldn't it?

Huge financial windfall for GetUp! Along with great publicity. It is almost as if Cory Bernardi condemned GetUp! Own goal by the government. The same will happen with SSM. So many more people registered to be on the electoral role and in reality these extra voters will see the government ousted come next election

The Turnbull government sets up and spruiks about commissions of enquiry. They say that these are the ideal way of developing policy and progress on difficult issues. Then when reports are given and recommendations made, it nitpicks these that match with its own ideology instead of looking at the reasoning behind them. We have had it in energy, child abuse and now first nation. Why don't they cut out the middleman officially and tell us what the report has to find that is acceptable? So much work goes into these and so much promise and expectation created and all for very little. The SSM survey will probably be seen as just window dressing too for a decision that has already been made.

So how do Ministers find out what is happening with the department and organisations under their responsibility.... by TV of course. However, they may mistake the 'reality show' of their job for The Game of Thrones. How long will Little Finger (Peter Dutton) last?

Here's a tip for the media. Cox Plate. Winx wins. Say no more.

If Winston Peters is the NZ kingmaker, then will Cash be the accused of regicide in Australia should Turnbull's Camelot tumble down?

The AFP had to respond to the search warrant authorisation. However, to do so with so many officers and in full gaze of alerted media is surely an operational matter and thus an operational mistake. Cash and others pressured the Registered Organisations Commission to act. The dominoes then fell, a search warrant was sought, a magistrate signed off on it and the AFP followed it through. It may be an arm's length approach but some political finger pushed those dominoes.

Will Cash's ex-employee use the unfair dismissal provisions...... oh that's right.... due to the revamp of legislation those provisions have been dismissed by Cash

What a shame that the timing of the Cash and Carry (the can) saga has hit when details of the response to the RC on child sexual abuse. This real news may be only able to make page 14 in the papers if it gets a run at all. There was enough good news in it for the government and also enough for the opposition to point out the shortcomings. Yet hardly a question on it will be asked today in Question Time I reckon.

Senator Cormann has forgotten that the Coalition party room is made entirely of glass. Put down those stones before you do more damage.

Somewhere in the constitution it must say that senators and MP's must be of sound mind. If so, there should be more cases brought before the High Court. No-one in their right mind would be doing what our politicians are currently doing.

Senator Cormann's response about Labor pushing a "blatant political agenda" is laughable after the raids. The shame is that that is what nearly all our reps in parliament do. They don't govern, they play politics and they are awful at that.

So, who is running the country? Not the ministers for sure. Decisions are being made by apparatchiks in back room offices under the unwatchful eye of those supposed to be in charge.

A premier resigns over a bottle of Grange but what does a Minister have to do? The ministerial code of conduct is slipping. The standards of the Westminster system are dropping as fast as house prices are rising

Cash is being toasted, roasted and grilled. She is eating humble pie with egg on her face and has now developed a sensitivity to leeks. At least she knows her onions unlike a former Prime Minister.

And we think our gun laws are okay. Employment Minister Cash has shot herself in the foot while her foot was in her mouth.

Has some collusion or arse covering been cooked up over lunch. Stay tuned.

The appointment of justices to the high court is supposed to be apolitical but they are appointed by the Governor General on advice from the Prime Minister. The process is simple really. The appointment lists are put forward to cabinet by the Attorney General and then the recommendations via the PM go to the Governor General. Currently four have been appointed by Liberal Prime Ministers and three by Labor Prime Ministers so if there is a dissenting ruling, one wonders whether it will be seen to be a political outcome.

I wonder whether Malcolm Roberts is quaking in his boots because he was relying on what has been discussed as sub judice? Perhaps he thinks now he misheard and it is what Judge Judy says.

Apparently, a truckload of wet lettuce has just been ordered for the High Court. Is a salad on their menu?

Let's see the logic that applies. We have seven people who help make laws in this country. These seven people, knowingly or otherwise have broken a law as laid out in the constitution. Are they above the law? Are they beyond the reach of the law? Should the law be reinterpreted just for them? If they are not found guilty, then can I use that judgement as a precedent for breaking the law? Oh, for the wisdom of Solomon.

The High Court is architecturally a brutalist building. Really? That's harsh. I thought anthropomorphising structures, particularly courts was passé. The people in the building determine the mood of the building or perhaps you have already judged them or their judgements.

Ah the munificent seven, giving up their time freely to serve the public. No. I am not talking about the malcontent seven at the high court but the volunteers at my local op shop who are there giving back more to the community than what the community has ever given them.

In 1975 we had the dismissal. Forty-two years on and all we have is the dismal.

So many leaks and the rats have nowhere to run to on the SS Turnbull. They sit there and hope that no-one else decides to drill a hole in the bottom to let the water out.

November

- President of the Senate Stephen Parry, Jacqui Lambie and John Alexander resign over dual citizenship issues
- The Turnbull government sets up the Royal Commission into Misconduct in the Banking, Superannuation and Financial Services Industry
- An earthquake strikes the border region between Iraq and Iran leaving at least 530 dead and over 70,000 homeless
- Zimbabwean President Robert Mugabe is placed under house arrest, as the military take control of the country. Mugabe resigns after 37 years as president
- A mosque attack in Sinai, Egypt kills 305 worshippers and leaves hundreds more wounded.
- Sam Dastyari forced to resign from his position due to alleged corruption and being influenced by Chinese spies.
- Same Sex Marriage Bill plebiscite conducted. Overwhelming yes vote by public.

On display were the underdeveloped minds of the overexposed politicians.

Scott Ludlam, Larissa Waters and Jacqui Lambie, when they first realised that they had an issue with dual citizenship immediately resigned. Others have stayed on and enjoyed the pay they were receiving under false pretences. There is no honour amongst thieves.

Imagine, someone new comes into the Parliament, without the formal obedience schooling of a major party, is not a political apparatchik, is not schooled in the law or parachuted in as a celebrity, then proceeds to make the same mistake about citizenship that more so-called eminent colleagues do. Should we be surprised? Not by her, but by the vanity and born to rule attitude

of those who should have done more due diligence if they were as good as they said they were.

So, another Newspoll bites the dust, the massive citizenship issues, the PM away...... and yet Tony has stayed silent. What a chance for a coup and he's missed it. That guy doesn't know his onions!

I didn't know that prorogue was a verb. I thought that it stood for the professional rogues who inhabit parliament.

They talk about the theatre of parliament but we are seeing is a comedic farce put on by (s)ham actors who haven't read the contract thoroughly and yet are still getting paid a fortune and reaping the spoils of stardom.

Senator James Paterson has probably boosted his chances with that snub from Malcolm 'on-the-nose' Turnbull. He should wear it as a badge of honour. The far right may now start grooming him as a potential leader.

Clive Palmer should have checked the vetting of his candidates but then again, he was probably busy deconstructing his links with a certain nickel mine.

Has anyone added up the primary votes the replacement senators received in the last election? It is a good thing they aren't in the House of Reps because they certainly don't represent very many people in their state. If the constitution ever gets changed then how about looking at how replacement senators are appointed.

And we were worried that the Chinese were coming in to buy up the place and run the country. Other foreigners have been doing that for years through parliament. Why does our constitution make us seem quite xenophobic? Please explain.

There needs to be sign where politicians enter Parliament House that reads:

Park your egos. Leave any wheelbarrows to be pushed outside. Take off any political party ideology and place it in the cloak room along with any sexism, racism or willingness to discriminate. Your

role here is not self-serving, nor is it to serve a party. You have a job to do on behalf of ALL Australians. You chose to be here and to do this job. Now just get on with it without any fanfare, fuss and self-aggrandisement.

"Mr Turnbull wants legislation passed by Christmas" He had the opportunity months ago and lacked the courage to do it. What part of his anatomy has the far right got hold of?

Just watch the likes of Abetz, Abbott, Andrews and Bernardi man the battlements armed only with filibuster and having nothing else but amendments in their arsenal. You will hear them when the SSM Bill is presented screaming, "Thou shall not pass"

The Bakers Association of Australia can see a pot of gold at the end of the rainbow. Good on the Bakers Association of Australia for saying "Let them eat cake!" With the Paterson Bill the far right want to have their cake and eat it too.

Senator Bernardi's vote on SSM will be interesting to say the least. 62.5% of South Australians voted yes and 37.5% voted no. There was an 80% turnout in South Australia. Will his Australian Conservatives party fall without ever winning a seat come next election?

Daylesford-Hepburn, the gay capital of Victoria, better start organising itself for an influx of wedding guests. Hope the venues, accommodation and reception centres are pre-planning. What a boost in economy for towns such as these all across Australia. A rainbow led recovery should make so many people smile.

Brandis may now seem to be getting a heart like the Tinman, but is still lacking in courage and brains when standing up to the right wing.

Will this new Senate, post citizenship debacle, be truly representative? Maybe that is why it isn't known as a a House of Representatives. How many primary votes did each senator get?

Perhaps Jacqui Lambie, that well-known Scot could have used William Wallace's quote as she left Parliament, "There's a difference between us. You think the people of this country exist to provide you with position. I think your position exists to provide those people with freedom."

Or the ones who voted no are soundly beaten when you add the yes and didn't vote numbers together. Those who chose not to vote can't be counted for either side. We know what we know only from those who chose to vote. 61.6% voted yes and 38.4% voted no Australia wide. 133 out of 150 electorates voted yes. Those who choose to massage figures need to be held to account because their numbers up.

Strangely enough homosexuality going against human nature is not true. Homosexuality has been part of most civilised and uncivilised cultures for as long as mankind has been around. Only in fairly recent history has it been seen by some cultures and religions as being abhorrent, a sin and even treated as a mental disorder.

Amazing how we live in a news cycle that has a short-lived focus. Are those people on Manus forgotten? Will Michaelia Cash ever have to explain what actually happened with the union raid? What citizenship issue? Yesterday's news is so well... er... um... yesterday.

How will senators vote as they represent states and territories? Every state and territory had a majority that voted yes, ranging from 58% (NSW) to 74% (ACT). Sounds like that if these people wish to stay representing their state or territory, it should be a unanimous vote. MHR's should vote according to their electorate. Isn't that how democracy should work? Those who don't follow the wishes of their electorates run a huge risk of future unemployment.

Will Tony vote against his own electorate's wishes? How many others will do the same? And what of Bennelong? No-one can vote for them. It will take a very brave person to tell an electorate that despite

75% of people voting Yes that a No vote is what will be delivered in parliament.

Over 120 million dollars to state the bleedin' obvious. We should recoup the money from those politicians who voted for a plebiscite.

Interesting use of Maths by some to say that the No vote was nearly 50%. They have assumed that those who didn't respond voted No. That is a mighty leap of faith but statistically improbable.

One interesting thing that will arise out of the SSM bill should it be put before parliament, is that a conscious vote will take place. What is sad is that every vote vote on the floor of parliament should be a conscious vote not one tied to the loudest voice in a party room. If parliamentarians are not choosing what is right for their electorate and Australia ahead of their party, then why are they there? Voting unconsciously, they might as well be asleep or perhaps in a drunken stupor on a couch somewhere.

So cast your mind back and list the Prime Ministers and Opposition Leaders who haven't been flawed and divisive. Such is the nature of adversarial parliamentary debates. Consensus is so hard to achieve with a political party entrenched system.

The Australian people will have in all probability responded seeking the end to another discriminatory practice. The Paterson bill however merely entrenches that discrimination. LGBTIQ people should be free to marry but Senator Paterson wants to curtail that freedom and allow bigotry to continue.

The campaign began way back years ago when John Howard changed the Marriage Act in 2004. It was a low act to reinforce outdated and outmoded beliefs. Today may be just the beginning of change and Australia may come of age. Being linked to a 1950's attitude does not do us well on the world stage and betrays the honour of ALL Australians. It will be a healthy sign if we can remove one more piece of discrimination from our culture.

When will people realise that to lead a country is an honour not a prize. Our current leader has sold his ethics, values and Australia out to the whims of the far right of his party. The same sex marriage plebiscite is but one example. All to achieve the prize of being the PM. What price honour? Somewhere in the Paradise papers there will be a payment of thirty pieces of silver. It will be well hidden but we know whose it is.

A Yes response is only one step. The politicians then have to agree to put a bill before Parliament, a bill that doesn't discriminate but merely rights a terrible wrong. Then it has to pass both houses intact without watering down what a Yes response was all about. Then all the nay-sayers need to back off and let people be allowed to feel free to marry if they wish. The latter will be the hardest part, but the others will also be difficult. Today is just a small step on the way and should show that Australians can be mature, free thinking and compassionate people.

Palaszczuk vetoing any loans from the Federal Government to Adani would be admitting she made a mistake when she lodged the application last year. How refreshing to find a politician willing to fess up to an error of judgement.

A sign outside parliament may see few on the floor. "Would all those who are feathering their own nests, please leave."

Malcolm says that the result of the Queensland election had nothing to do with federal politics and then in the next sentence admonishes Queensland One Nation voters saying they need to rethink or there won't be a federal coalition government. He wants it both ways.

Why do these Beatles lyrics of Nowhere Man remind me about Malcolm Turnbull perhaps because he "doesn't have a point of view and knows not where he's going to.........."

The time has come to see if Senators truly represent their states. All states and territories had a majority of Yes voters. Let's see if Senators have any honour.

Zed Seselja said that the 'no' voters must be respected' yet by imposing massive restrictions he is actually disrespecting the wishes of the majority of Australians who resoundingly voted Yes.

If we can't refuse service to individual LGBQIT people or to anyone based on race, colour, culture etc. Why should it be okay to do so to LGBQIT couples? Or are suddenly just those couples to be made exempt from the anti-discrimination act? Seems an act of malice by sore losers.

One Nation's orange has suddenly not become the new black.

So, if the government decides that the House of Reps shouldn't sit this week, is that technically a lock out situation? Perhaps Fair Work Australia will be called on to investigate. Probably not because they work on the principle of a fair day's work for a fair day's pay and that certainly doesn't apply to politicians.

Will Turnbull survive until Christmas? That's the $40,000 question.

I'm not from the IPA, but I suggest that you would be better off registering as a religious organisation rather than as a charitable organisation. Then you pay no tax, no rates, can attract subsidies and can say and do as you like.

Instead of meekly accepting Abbott's analysis of a "faustian pact", why didn't someone counter with asking about his own Machiavellian connivings?

Over two thousand years ago, it is said, a lowly carpenter led his heavily pregnant wife into a town but there was no room at the inn and the couple were forced to seek shelter in a stable. All these years later little has changed. Australia is the inn and there is no room for the Nauru and Manus Island refugees. What a 'Christian' civilised nation we are.

"The era of the political assassination has to end" should be followed by the words 'et tu brute'

A couple of weeks to go before we find out whether Alexander is not so great.

I wonder with these hours of speeches that the Senate and House of Reps will go through, whether the politicians will remember that the people have already spoken.

Pride is such as foul-tasting thing in politics. No party is willing to swallow it. They would rather fall on their sword than accept that they may have been wrong and the other side right. Even Tony Abbott said that no-one was the suppository of all wisdom and he was up himself. Surely a Royal Commission into banking would clear the air and show that the Turnbull government actually listened to their constituents and not to big business.

Matt Canavan thinks that by admonishing his colleagues publicly on television will bring them back into the fold on a Royal Commission on Banking. That will be just as effective as Christopher Pyne's telling them that disunity is death.

Is anyone offering odds that Barnaby Joyce will do the haka as a greeting to his colleagues if and when he greets them again in the coalition party room?

Bennelong election campaign. For John Alexander it must seems it's Been-a-long election campaign.

Climate change can't be denied. Even the Hottest 100 has moved forward.

Malcolm Turnbull has been attending leaders' conferences overseas. Why? A bit underqualified isn't he, after all what experience at leadership has he demonstrated?

Figures in from the Medicare Review Committee indicate that Canberra is a place where a lot of unwarranted procedures are taking place. Brain scans that show nothing. Open heart surgery where no heart is apparently there. Even ethical bypasses are being claimed against the public purse.

Did the Russians influence Australian elections and thus Pauline Hanson was elected? If so, it just shows the Russians DO have a sense of humour.

If the Senate passes the SSM legislation early as expected, it could work on legislation that the House of Reps passed early this week...... What do you mean the House of Reps has called a week-long sickie???? The cricket finished early.

The truth is if you say something often enough it looks like it is true. The truth is if you say something often enough it looks like it is true. The truth is if you say something often enough it looks like it is true. The truth is if you say something often enough it looks like it is true.

Two very special pieces of legislation have really shown what politics should be about. In Victoria the assisted dying laws and federally the same sex marriage laws show that politicians do care about real things and not just economics, ideologies and themselves.

You can't really claim to represent the silent majority. How do you know what they all believe if they don't tell anyone? It would be like saying that everyone who didn't vote in the SSM survey really said no. A true democracy is one where every voice is heard and everyone casts a vote. Pauline Hanson does not represent the silent majority. She represents a certain number of Queenslanders who voted for her and her party. As a Senator she is there to represent all of Queensland

It shouldn't be Christopher Pyne, but the Chief Coalition whip who should be discreetly chastising colleagues. Oh, that's right she is a little bit busy at the moment with her 'dual' roles.

Oh, if only the ABC had enough money in its budget to allow more proper political analysis. But sadly, their money has been

diverted to provide assistance in the form of infrastructure promises to have Coalition members re-elected.

Christopher Pyne must have splinters in a painful area from sitting on the fence that divides two camps. He says, "The reality is we don't have a Stalinist approach to these things - one of the things that makes us a better party is that we respect the rights of individual members to cross the floor to exercise their conscience." then proceeds to tell his colleagues not to do it because "disunity is death". It seems that we have had so much disunity in all parties over the past ten years that we are being feted by zombies at elections and by-elections.

Let's see what rights the 'them' (Indigenous Australians) have.

***The right to a higher infant mortality.**

***The right to have higher incarceration rates.**

***The right to a shorter life span.**

***The right to live below the poverty line.**

*** The right to have their tribal lands taken away from them.**

*** The right to a second rate education.**

*** The right to not be properly acknowledged in the Constitution.**

Glad Pauline is fighting for the same rights for other Australians.

I propose that we have a Royal Commission into Royal Commissions. Some of the terms of reference would be:

(1) the inordinate cost

(2) the politics being played to set them up, particularly when it targets individual opponents

(3) the length of time they take to complete

(4) the lack of action by governments on most of the recommendations

(5) and whether the Queen actually does take a commission from the whole process. Surely

she is rich enough already.

The Senate has become an echo chamber. How many senators have actually sat in and listened to other speakers on the same sex marriage bill debate? Hardly any. Does anyone actually work in Canberra or does everyone in Canberra think that they have earned a week-long weekend?

I smell pork in the air around Bennelong. Malcolm Turnbull has announced a $100 million-odd transport hub for the seat. What a crackling contest this seat has become!

Has the good ship, Coalition Policies, hit a reef? It seems to be foundering and the rats disembarking. Or is it just a ghost ship that never really existed?

Little is happening and nothing being achieved this week in the House of Reps. A normal week in Canberra.

Because of our banks' potential exposure during the GFC, the government was forced to guarantee underwriting them. Since then they have prospered enormously. It is about time they gave something back since their recovery. The government should just call their bluff and withdraw that guarantee but we have had weak and ineffectual economic managers since Keating and Costello.

The public seem to be losing interest in the banking system. Someone should look into that.

Some say that Turnbull is the gift that keeps giving for the Labor Party but he's more like pass the parcel. The more you unwrap, the smaller and more inconsequential the contents seem to be.

The marketing of the NBN is very clever. They sell you an inferior product that is literally not up to speed. If you have difficulties you can email them from your non-working computer, call them on their hotline from a landline that is now faulty, or pay a fortune to be put on hold paying expensive mobile charges until someone offers their only worthwhile option saying, "Have you tried turning it off and turning it on again". I may join all the others in line who are raiding their cutlery drawers for something to use on the whizz kid who came up with fibre to the node concept. I understand that even members of his own party are in that queue. I am prepared to wait for my turn. Can't take as long as waiting for my internet to work properly can it?

So, the main role of a member is to what? Can't be to represent the views of the majority of their electorate surely or the SSM bill would have been passed by the Senate unanimously.

My local Chinese restaurant serves money bags as entrees. Can see how Sam got confused.

George Brandis should note that true leadership is when a government knows what the majority of Australians want and need and then has the courage to make it happen. True leadership is not delaying things with a non-compulsory expensive plebiscite that some Senators ignored anyway. It is about knowing what direction to go, taking your head out of the sand and actually showing people the way ahead. So many in the Liberal party have acted as if they were auditioning for the cowardly lion role in a remake of the Wizard of Oz.

Have we just won the America's Cup? One Prime Minister once said when that happened "Any boss who sacks anyone for not turning up today is a bum" Malcolm Turnbull has told everyone in the House of Reps not to turn up. So, have I missed a yachting news story?

Let's hope that the debating en-masse that the House of Reps on SSM next week isn't televised. That would look horrible. Just tell us the final vote numbers and who opted to vote against the wishes of their own electorate.

Can you see the Coalition setting up a Royal Commission into the Dastyari affair? Hardly likely because so many other politicians of all persuasions would come under scrutiny with snout in the trough disease.

According to a dictionary definition a majority would be anything over 50%. By my reckoning adding another 10% to that would be significant. If I got a pay rise of 10% THAT would be significant.

Talk about inflation! Thirty pieces of silver now equates to $40,000.

Behind every dark (NO) cloud there is a silver (YES) lining. Today's is even better with a glorious rainbow shining with it.

Perhaps Sam has Asperger syndrome. No, wait! Someone else has used that implausible excuse this week.

Here's a multiple choice quiz:

If I decide to form a religious organisation, I can

a) have major tax concessions in running the organisation.

b) actively discriminate against who I like about what I like.

c) not only set up my own indoctrinating schools, but get government funding to do so.

d) give my supporters the opportunity to minimise their taxes by donating money to my organisations.

e) all of the above.

Has someone Shanghaied Sam's loyalty?

Listening to some senators you wonder why they got elected in the first place. A backroom meeting of some power brokers in a party put them on a ticket and then we vote for the party not sure just what we are getting. Our ignorance sees ignoramuses making ignorant statements in the Senate.

The problem about long serving senators and members of the house of reps is that they have learnt all the tricks to delay and defeat good legislation. Instead of analysing the merits of each bill and amendments proposed if any, they spend so much time soothing their own egos by grandstanding and inflating their own self-importance. They are public servants and isn't it about time they served the public and not themselves.

I may be wrong but is Simon Birmingham the sort of option as PM that many Australians would accept. Shame he is in the Senate.

Sam Dastyari..... an early Christmas present for Malcolm. And he was just thinking that all he was getting was coal (from Adani possibly) in his Christmas stocking.

Senator Ian MacDonald needs to reflect on his religious upbringing. The words from Luke 6:38 come to mind "Give, and it Will be Given to You".

They say that our major cities are becoming so light at night that it is hard to see the milky way. There must be a black hole over Parliament House in Canberra because even though our best and brightest are definitely not there, there are no stars to be seen at all.

I hope all those politicians who took the week off bring a note explaining their absence, one that is not signed 'Epstein's mother'. Such excuses as 'I was helping a mate get re-elected' should be rejected out of hand.

Perhaps there should be ethics classes taught for all politicians. The threshold would need to be a 100% pass mark to qualify them for sitting in parliament. Perhaps when the constitution gets changed regarding section 44 that requirement could be added. Although that may not work as most politicians seem to renounce their ethics once elected.

Sam would have been better off declaring dual citizenship to avoid such public scrutiny. But then he couldn't. Dual refers to two and, by my count, Australia, Iran and China make three.

Poor Sam. He would never be picked to play for the Socceroos in Russia - too many own goals. Now if the World Cup was in China......

Sam should have demanded the cone of silence when he was talking to Huang.

All Sam had to do was to tell the Chinese that they should use VOIP on the NBN. He would have been seen as a double agent and receive accolades from the Senate for stuffing up Chinese spy communication networks.

Sam's explanation would have made more sense if he had worn a trench coat, dark glasses, fedora hat and a furtive look.

It would be impossible for Sam to leak any intelligent information. That would mean he had intelligence.

I think that everyone is being piggist in their comments.

The Labor party 'trying to make a silk purse out of a sow's ear'

Politicians with their 'snouts in the trough',

'Brandis happy as a 'pig in mud' over Datyari's stuff up

'Pigs will fly' before some politicians admit they have made a mistake.

The agreeing to the fibre to the node of the NBN was like 'buying a pig in a poke'

Bill thinking his zingers are like 'casting pearls before swine'.

Pollies living 'high on the hog' while they make a 'pig's ear' of running the country.

If I ask you nice to stop you are likely to say 'pig's arse' I will, so I will just remind you how boaring you are.

Bank shares are nosediving after the announcement of a royal commission. What does that tell us? Banks have got something to hide and may be exposed to future financial litigation? Perhaps bank share prices were as over-inflated as much as credit card fees?

So how do banks work? They take money from people and offer to mind it and then give a small amount of interest back. They then lend that money to others who pay huge interest and charges. The bank pockets the difference between the pittance that is paid to depositors and the exorbitant amounts paid by borrowers. Someone remind me of the meaning of usury again.

We spent $122 million to let politicians know that there should be same sex marriage. Now we are spending $75 million to let politicians know that the banks have been rorting the system and

the public for years. Such things should be self-evident. However, let's hope that the government will act as swiftly on the royal commission findings as they are trying to do on SSM.

'Voices from the Past' Does he also have a sixth sense and see dead people too? I think not. The word non-sense comes to mind when I hear the name Abetz.

Abbott has a lot to answer for. He took his opposition tactics into Government and Dr No and his successor have been unable to change. The Coalition should act as if they were in government, boldly stating what they have done and what they will do rather than what the Labor Party would do if they were in power. If they continue down this path, the Labor Party WILL be in power shortly. Leaders should lead rather than say why others shouldn't lead. Howard for all the bad things he did such as the Iraq War involvement, actually led. Before him, Keating, Hawke, Fraser and Whitlam also had the courage of their convictions and led. Turnbull and Abbott will appear alongside Billy McMahon behind even Rudd and Gillard near the bottom of the list of greatest Prime Ministers of Australia.

Now we know that MT promises are really empty promises. SSM will be delayed. His salve to the consciences of certain disaffected Coalition colleagues by agreeing to a royal commission won't be enough. They will have gained confidence and press for a huge array of amendments to the SSM bill

So technically speaking has Malcolm done a backflip or a bankflip?

Interesting to note that adroit means: skilful, adept, dexterous, deft, agile, and nimble. Yet maladroit means: awkward, inept, clumsy, bumbling, incompetent, unskilful, inexpert, graceless and cloddish.

So for Turnbull it depends where the space is. Is Mal adroit or is he maladroit?

Imagine how much higher the average IQ of the Labor Party Senate team will rise should Sam completely resign from the Senate or be cast adrift from the Labor Party and move to the crossbench. If the latter occurred, he could always sit next to Pauline and they could audition for the next Dumb and Dumber movie.

Just how far down the Labor Party's NSW senate ticket will Sam be next election? Talk about a fall from grace.

The Finance Minister should also have been at the Press Conference. I would have loved to hear him say that they were not vibble vobbling.

Malcolm is not calling the royal commission into banking because it is needed, but "This is an inquiry that is necessary given the circumstances of the time." i.e. he hasn't the numbers on the floor. My only question is from which of his two faces did the words emanate from?

It seems that Section 44 of the constitution will claim another victim. The unwritten part vi) which says "does completely stupid things."

Sam may be referred to the High Court for not renouncing his idiocy.

However, based on what we have seen, many more MP's may be forced to resign over this same provision.

Turnbull was backed into a corner and forced to do the right thing rather than have the humiliation of watching his coalition colleagues cross the floor to achieve the same results. The broad church that is the Liberal Party has so many corners. They are not done with Turnbull yet.

If the CEOs of the Commonwealth, Westpac, National Australia and ANZ banks made the request in an email sent on Thursday to Treasurer Scott Morrison then how can he then say that the banks were not told of the royal commission "until this very

minute" Seems the tail is wagging the dog but the dog doesn't want
to admit it.

Malcolm's Thursday morning breakfast menu was a choice of

Oeuf sur le visage

Or

2) Amende honorable

(For those not used to French restaurant menus this translates to

Egg on face

Or

2)Humble pie)

Either way he is toast.

The only person standing between Bill Shorten and the Prime
Ministership hasn't gone far enough. Sam Dastyari should have quit
the Senate completely.

**Blinded by the light of either his own ego or ideology, Turnbull
has finally seen the light that was actually at the end of the long
dark tunnel of his leadership. The oncoming train approaching at
the next election however is going in the opposite direction.**

So, Malcolm said, "The potential for such an inquiry is starting
to undermine confidence" when referring to a royal commission into
banking. Sad to say the confidence had already been undermined by the
banks' own actions and their inordinate profiteering at the expense of
customers and customer service.

With apologies to Talking Heads

"Sam's on the road to Nowhere

He's had to resign

The wording was in Chinese

He couldn't read the signs"

December

- Barnaby Joyce wins the New England by-election
- Final report, including recommendations, of the Royal Commission into Institutional Responses to Child Sexual Abuse is handed to government
- The United States officially recognizes Jerusalem as Israel's capital
- The Iraqi military announces that it has "fully liberated" all of Iraq's territory from "ISIS terrorist gangs" and retaken full control of the Iraqi-Syrian border
- Same Sex Marriage Bill passed

Tim Wilson proposing in Parliament is like having the wedding banns read at church. He now has to wait to see if there are objections from the congregation. He'll be praying that everyone says yes just as his partner did.

Is Barnaby sounding repetitious? Absolutely, absolutely. (It's contagious)

So, someone is running an escort service for Barnaby Joyce........... the image is not a good one but it will stay in your memories for a long time now it has been said.

Today we will find out if what Aristophanes said is true, "Characteristics of a popular politician: a horrible voice, bad breeding, and a vulgar manner."

Fifteen hours of debate!! What's the bet it is all talk and no action. Bring on the amendments as soon as possible and vote on them straight away. Every politician will be out to justify to their electorate why they are voting the way they are. It will be either bravery or stupidity to vote contrary to what their electorate said in the survey. When we are talking about politicians, I am thinking the latter.

I may be asking stupid questions but how did the secret recordings of Sam Dastyari become public? Who made them? Who leaked them? Surely some staffer will be Cashed out soon because that is how governments deal with such issues.

Bells have started ringing, we await the news
After MP's express their views
Same sex marriage is on the agenda again
No one knows when the talking will end
Don't care if it takes all night
As long as they do what is right
Get it done by Christmas
Just get it done for Christmas.......
(apologies to The Eagles)

The only Pole I am interested in is the results at the North Pole. Is Santa cashed up because a lot of workers certainly aren't with flat wages growth and soaring energy costs? Coal may be all the Coalition deserve (and probably are really happy to have) in their stockings this year.

How many senators and reps will seek an extension of time or say the dog ate their homework? Section 44 has five parts to it. There could be a need for new paving between Parliament House and the High Court.

With the numbers in the House precarious, will Malcolm be able to manage a Huang parliament? Probably, because anyone who donates equally to both sides of politics can't possibly lose.

"How did it all come to this?" the people who originally wrote the constitution must be thinking as they are rolling in their graves. The country's wealth and prosperity has been squandered and sold off to the highest bidder and now the bidders are back buying up the pledges of politicians.

Forget the High Court. Establish a proper Federal ICAC and cast out and/or gaol those lobbyists and politicians from all sides of politics who are corrupt.

You would think a certain right-wing shock jock would lisp with that forked tongue of his. He conveniently forgets the amount of money donated by the Chinese to the Coalition coffers at the last election.

So, Barnaby represents New England. Is that the one pre-Brexit or post-Brexit? Does that make him still have section 44 issues?

Will just Dastyari be caught by the smoking Huang? Lots of people have been willing to sell their souls for some election money from this Chinese businessman.

Malcolm Turnbull 'rejoyced' in Barnaby's win, not just because the numbers in the house seem a bit better, nor because he now has his deputy PM back, but simply because he now has someone who can almost control the rag tag group that are the Nationals.

If someone in Labor changes policy such as the Queensland premier regarding Adani, then that is tantamount to treason. However, if a Coalition member changes policy such as a PM on a banking royal commission, then that is showing wise political judgement. Double standards from two faced hypocrites maybe?

Like to see Turnbull's evidence that qualifies Andrew Robb for sainthood

Hypocrisy thy name is Liberal. Both parties have in the past courted overseas money. Money that has to come with strings attached and thus we have puppet governments.

If One Nation wants Australia to become one nation, surely such a divisive character being lauded by that party is counterproductive.

The government can't complain about the extended sitting hours. The bill passed the senate mid-week last week but it couldn't be looked at in the house because Malcolm gave everyone the week off. Someone should take the politics out of government. They play games with people's lives and don't understand that their immaturity causes them to be held in contempt by a lot of the general public.

Disunity is death according to Christopher Pyne. Failing to turn up to a division could be the beginnings of a fatal disease. It beggars belief that someone who hasn't heard what a motion or a bill is all about, weighed up the arguments that were spoken on the floor of the house is allowed to rush in and vote anyway.

Why does the party in government control the agenda entirely? Surely there must be a way for other parties to put up proposed bills and have them added to the agenda without the Manager for Government Business saying, "Move on, nothing to see here" or completely jamming the agenda so that no-one else gets a look in.

If only those people on Manus had a son who won a Brownlow, they'd be here in Oz quicksmart without ruby slippers.

Wouldn't matter really if Labor had no policies. All they have to do is say they are not the Coalition and they win in the polls. Talent and policies lacking on all sides.

100 speakers yet to say whether they thought that their electorates were right or wrong. Did Malcolm specify which Christmas the bill would pass by?

"We will decide who comes into our country." I would take 600 people from Manus ahead of Milo Yiannopoulos on a speaking tour.

Confucius say, "Man worried about mobile phone should not put in pocket set on vibrate just in case of unintended outcome. Better to leave in house.

Looking at what the alt-right cause in terms of dividing a nation you see what a difference Milo makes.

On the cricket field Australia wins, but in Parliament Australia loses almost every day.

And the SSM debate is at what stage? I'm bored with the other stuff.

China is getting Robbed!

Maybe the general populace could crowd fund the taking of ALL politicians to the High Court and get it over and done with.

How many dogs has Feeney got? How do they survive eating just his homework? Call the RSPCA!!!

There's nothing more interesting than someone protecting their self-interest. That of course takes precedence over good policy and representing your electorate for politicians. It is all about them, them, them. Bugger the rest of the community

"A prime minister washed up and swept away without a trace," Mr Turnbull's epilogue will read.

They say if you pay peanuts you get monkeys. Given the amount of money our politicians earn and their sub-standard performance, when did the price of peanuts go through the roof? I'd invest in peanuts rather than Bitcoins if I were you.

Turnbull lost badly by voting against the Labor motion to refer nine to the High Court. He could have put the citizenship saga behind him and seen to be non-partisan. Shorten played him well. His motion was a win-win for him. Now Turnbull has to make a move and anything he does now will not be viewed well by the public who are sick of the whole saga and just want their politicians to focus on their jobs. Not their own security but properly representing their electorate. Politicians have dipped below Used Car Salespeople lawyers and Real Estate Agents in their standing in the community by the general public. However, from there the only way is up I guess.

Perhaps we need to divest more power to the High Court and give them the right to investigate without referral into the politicians who may not meet constitutional requirements.

If Labor's motion failed by one vote, how many on the hit list voted? Hopefully they abstained from voting.

Milo Yiannopoulos - yesterday's news now fish and chip wrapping in a certain person's old fish and chip shop. Irony is delightful.

Should we rename what ensues after an MP is found ineligible to sit in the house? My vote is for a "kiss them good" by-election.

How many left to speak on SSM? Santa is watching and we need to see who is naughty and who is nice.

Let's get rid of the unfair dismissal laws so that we can sack our politicians before their tenure is up.

How many politicians caught up in the dual citizenship chaos have handled themselves with dignity and humility? How many have not blamed the constitution but blamed themselves for lack of due diligence? I'd like to suggest Scott Ludlam and Larissa Waters as starters. Jacqui Lambie probably deserves a mention too.

Will Barnaby be red faced and a bit sheepish because he cost taxpayers a fortune for not doing his homework. Or will he go at it like a bull at a gate as usual?

"Congratulations to all the Australians who went out a got a job," says ScoMo but he says it as he sits amongst people who are in a job they weren't qualified to be in.

Unemployment figures will rise post High Court decisions.

Andrew Robb - Money for nothing and trips for free! Why isn't he in Dire Straits?

How can John Alexander get his citizenship of Britain renounced so quickly i.e. within a week and others had theirs delayed for more than a month? It seems it may be who you know or maybe an intervention by Sir Humphrey Appleby wanna-be.

Will Sukkar also move an amendment that says thou shalt love thy neighbour? Think of all those neighbours on Manus that Dutton doesn't love

You wouldn't trust any of our politicians to run a chook raffle so why do we let them run the country?

Don't you just love parliamentary privilege where politicians can call anyone anything and get away with it, except they can't call each other liars, even though they may well be.

Seems that Bill Shorten's "no doubt" utterance holds as much water as Malcolm Turnbull's "And the High Court will so hold."

Do politicians get paid overtime? We mere PAYE taxpayers get paid over time. The time however is a fortnight but the wage amount is for a week.

As PM Abbott wouldn't change his pre-conceived ideas and got shafted. He has campaigned on the SSM issue with his own preconceived ideas and now has the hide to ask others to do what he was and still is unwilling to do.

Has Trump taken over Israel? He has now declared Israel's capital to be Jerusalem. I think that he takes the notion of being the leader of the free world too far. However, if he is that good can he declare that Manus Island Detention Centre is the capital of Australia and all the detainees there are entitled to the same rights as all Australians. I'd love to see our politicians running the country from there in those facilities.

It's the beginning of the end of the debate on same sex marriage. Some make it out to be the end of everything but for the majority it is the beginning of everything that is right for this world.

The Australian Characters

Tony Abbott
    Anthony Albanese
    Cory Bernardi
    Bronwyn Bishop
    Julie Bishop
    George Brandis
    Michaelia Cash
    Mathias Cormann
    Peter Dutton
    Josh Frydenberg
    Julia Gillard
    Pauline Hanson
    Joe Hockey
    Barnaby Joyce
    Craig Kelly
    Jacqui Lambie
    Michael McCormack
    Scott Morrison
    Clive Palmer
    Christopher Pyne
    Kevin Rudd
    Bill Shorten
    Angus Taylor
    Malcolm Turnbull
    Penny Wong

Tony Abbott

Tony Abbott was a very divisive person who rose to Opposition leader after being a minister in an earlier Coalition government. He rose even higher to become Prime Minister. As Opposition leader he was masterful and opposed almost everything that the government put forward. He was also very divisive within his own party ousting Opposition leader Malcolm Turnbull who repaid the favour by ousting him after Abbott became PM. A member of the right wing, Tony Abbott opposed Marriage Equality and Climate Change, denying the later saying that it was 'crap'. He defended big business, refusing to call a Royal Commission into banking and saying that 'Coal was good for humanity'. One of his strangest decisions was to reinstall knighthoods and knight Prince Phillip. After losing the Prime Ministership, he moved to the backbench promising not to undermine and snipe, yet that is precisely what he did and assisted in ousting PM Turnbull. Eventually he was beaten in the 2019 election and his blue-ribbon Liberal seat became an independent one.

Anthony Albanese

A very popular member on the Labor side of politics, Anthony Albanese was narrowly defeated by Bill Shorten as he attempted to become Opposition Leader. After Bill Shorten's defeat in the 2019 election, he was elected Opposition leader. A normally quietly spoken person some believe that he does not have the strength to win an election.

Cory Bernardi

Cory Bernardi as a senator from South Australia for the Liberal Party helped swing the party even further to the right especially on such issues as marriage equality and acceptance of any gender issues including the teaching of sex education in schools. He made the statement that homosexual relationships were just a step away from having sex with animals. A strong fundamentalist Christian he was against abortion and railed against Islam and the immigration of Muslims into Australia and met with ultra-right-wing advocates from overseas. He believed that the ABC as a broadcaster should have its funding reviewed if it continued to express views other than his own. In 2017 just after winning his seat as a Liberal, he split from the Liberal Party to form his own Conservative Party. This party of one eventually failed and he returned to the Liberal fold before announcing his retirement from Parliament in 2020.

Bronwyn Bishop

As Speaker in the House of Representatives who is supposed to be unbiased when making rulings, Bronwyn Bishop ruled with an iron fist and that fist was always on her right hand. The left side, the non-Coalition one, took the brunt of the force she exuded in the position of power she held. She set a record for the number of people she ejected from the chamber. Her position became untenable however because she claimed travel expenses of $5000 for a private helicopter flight to travel 80km to a Liberal party function.

Julie Bishop

Julie Bishop held the deputy leader position for the Liberal government from the time it went into Opposition in 2007 and saw four male colleagues come and go as leader of the party. She was a Minister between 2003 and 2007 and again from 2013 to 2018 when she was Minister for Foreign Affairs. A forthright speaker, she was known for her 'death stare', fashion sense and rarely seen dry sense of humour.

George Brandis

Known as 'Bookshelf Brandis' because of the very large and expensive bookshelves he had installed in his parliamentary office to store all his legal books, George Brandis served as a minister in the dying days of the Howard Government in 2007. From 2013 to 2015 he was made Attorney-General and Minister for the Arts, during which time he cut $105 million from the arts budget. He was left out of the ministry in 2015 but became Leader of the Government in the Senate. He was given a retirement gift of the High Commissionership in London in 2017. He was hailed by all sides of politics for the speech he gave condemning Pauline Hanson's wearing of a burka in the Senate.

Michaelia Cash

Michaelia Cash has seemed out of her depth in whatever portfolios she has been involved in. Accident prone and lacking in the understanding of what her powers are, she has been involved I many gaffes and abuses of power. Prime Ministers have nt known where to hide her. In one case, her staffers did their best and shielded her from questions by the media with a whiteboard. She has beautifully coiffed hair that shows that she is ding her best to delete the ozone layer. As speaker she is very good for the deaf as her lip movements are exaggerated. George H Bush may have said "Read my lips", but with Michaelia Cash, her lips seem to work on their own.

Mathias Cormann

Mathias Cormann held many positions in government and in opposition. His Belgian accent made him sound like Arnold Schwarzenegger but his dry wit and intelligence easily surpassed anything Schwarzenegger had to offer. He was articulate as Leader of the Government in the Senate and often called upon to argue strongly in the public arena on money matters. He served time as Finance Minister and was caught out smoking cigars with Joe Hockey at the time of the budget from hell. When leadership spills occurred as Malcolm Turnbull jockeyed to keep his position, he misread the situation and changed sides which ultimately led to the ascension of Scott Morrison.

Peter Dutton

Unfortunately blessed with the face of a funeral director, Peter Dutton has wielded power in the immigration/home affairs portfolio with the same compassionless façade. His ministry's powers have grown as has his standing within the Liberal Party despite his often poor timed and poor choice of words. He challenged for the leadership against Malcolm Turnbull and on the second challenge felt confident he would win and become PM, only to be undercut by Scott Morrison. A member of the right wing of the government he still manages to steer the government away from a centralist course and often is accused of speaking too much outside his portfolio.

Josh Frydenberg

As a relatively young person Josh Frydenberg moved up the ladder quite quickly to the point where he became deputy leader of the Liberal party and the country's treasurer. His main claim to fame he hopes will be delivering a surplus. However, he should be credited for the work he did to almost secure as Energy Minister an agreement between all parties for an emissions and energy policy. This was ultimately rolled when the right wing of his party forced a spill of leadership and Malcom Turnbull was dumped.

Julia Gillard

Julia Gillard became Australia's first female Prime Minister after Kevin Rudd lost in a leadership spill. She was also one of the most successful ones, managing to pass a lot of legislation despite having a hung parliament and relying on independents to get things through. Her biggest lack of success was in getting an emissions policy through and the scheme that was put forward was blocked by the Opposition who thought it unnecessary and strangely by the Greens who said that it didn't go far enough. Her statement that "there will be no carbon tax under the government I lead" gave the opposition all it needed even though her proposal wasn't a tax at all. It was believed that she was a lame duck going into the next election and a spill saw Kevin Rudd return as PM. She is credited for her beginning the Royal Commission into child abuse which saw many changes in society and ultimately the gaoling of priests and even a cardinal, George Pell. Her misogynism speech in parliament in 2012 aimed directly at Tony Abbott was lauded by women and many men all around the world.

Pauline Hanson

Originally elected to the senate in 1996 as an independent after being earlier taken off the Liberal Party ticket because of her racist views, Pauline Hanson is very right wing and accident prone when it comes to speaking and stunts. She lost her seat, was gaoled and then returned to the senate in 2007, this time not targeting Aborigines and Asians in her maiden speech but instead Muslims. She has been able to manipulate governments as her party One Nation has had balance of power opportunities in the Senate. Her party has had members come and go, some being more outlandish, some finding her views and control too hard to take. Her biggest and strangest stunts, gaffes and speeches have included responding to a question on xenophobia with "Please explain?" indicating she didn't know what it meant; wearing a burka into the senate; having her party associated with the NRA; speaking at ultra-right wing rallies; and releasing a video saying that she had been murdered.

Joe Hockey

Joe Hockey served as a minister in the Howard government from 2001 until 2007 and then became treasurer when the Coalition resumed power in 2013. His handling of the treasury portfolio and the 2014 'horror' budget in particular when he described Australians as 'lifters or leaners' saw him lose his portfolio when Malcolm Turnbull became PM. He retired from parliament only to become Australia's ambassador to the US in what seemed a payoff for services not rendered and also something he was not really qualified to do. Nicknamed "Smokin' Joe" by his enemies after he was caught puffing on a huge cigar with Mathias Cormann, this shadow treasurer who claimed that there was a debt and deficit emergency prior to the 2013 election managed to increase that deficit and debt in his short reign as treasurer.

Barnaby Joyce

He started as a senator in 2005 and in 2013 moved to the Lower House. He was often described as the best retail politician in the Coalition but when he became a minister in 2013 and then leader of the Nationals in 2018, things began to go awry. As a senator he threatened to and did cross the floor but as a cabinet minister he was not supposed to. His maverick persona was dulled. From a rural electorate he was supposed to represent what rural people wanted but that wasn't always the case because he towed the Coalition line. Caught up in the dual citizenship issue he had to recontest his seat and was successful. Best known for his ability to shout, his beetroot red face and his extra marital affair that cost him his position, he was one of those who undermined Malcolm Turnbull.

Craig Kelly

A person with strong right-wing views, Craig Kelly wields a lot of power from the backbench. An avid climate change denier and supporter of coal mining, he speaks out on these issues much to the annoyance of his fellow members of the Coalition. He threatened to join the cross bench if he was challenged for preselection and this bullying tactic worked as he was not challenged and held his seat in the 2019 election.

Jacqui Lambie

Jacqui Lambie is a former defence member and was elected to parliament under the Clive Palmer United Party platform as a senator. Following a fall out with Clive Palmer she became an outspoken independent senator who held the balance of power in the Senate. She had to recontest her seat after being found to have dual citizenship and was successful. She shoots straight and from the hip and horse-trades to get her way on many things.

Michael McCormack

He would rather be known as an important politician than an Elvis impersonator, sadly he is good at neither of those. He was the bland leader needed for the Nationals after the demise of Barnaby Joyce. His vacant look and his boring monotone seem to be a genuine reflection of his personality and his Coalition colleagues and indeed the Opposition as well as many members of the public are genuinely concerned when the PM leaves the country and Michael McCormack is left in charge.

Scott Morrison

In 2018, Scott Morrison seemed surprised when all those around him fell and he became Prime Minister. However, some say that it was heavily planned by his supporters. He set up a masterful campaign, creating himself as the person front and centre, and had few policies to criticise thus he was able to narrowly win the unwinnable election in 2019. Having worked in the tourism industry in New Zealand and Australia where he "left" both these positions before his contract was up, he moved into politics in 2007 and made his way quickly into a shadow ministry position. He became Immigration Minister in 2013 introducing sovereign borders policies and denying the media and public to information on asylum seekers and their detention on Christmas Island, Nauru and Manus Island. In 2014 he was moved to Social Services Minister and then when Malcolm Turnbull became PM, Morrison became Treasurer, a position he held until he became Prime Minister. One Question time in Parliament he brought in a lump of coal as a prop and told the Opposition not to be scared of it. His Pentecostal faith he has raised front and centre and this has left him open to criticism. He made horrendous errors of judgement at the end of 2019 and at the beginning of 2020 when the whole east coast of Australia was hit by bushfires. Taking a holiday to Hawaii at the time seemed to show lack of leadership and even on his return his performance was gaffe ridden. A strong supporter of the coal industry and a climate sceptic, he continues to paint a rosy picture of the country's ability to meet emissions targets. Any criticism of him or any of his colleagues he takes the line of "that's just the Canberra bubble" or he obfuscates, changes the topic, won't answer the question or lies. He has earned the nickname as "Scotty from Marketing" but he much prefers Scomo.

Clive Palmer

Clive Palmer first captured the centre of public attention when as a millionaire with mining interests he decided to splash out on building a full-sized working replica of the Titanic in 2012. Before that he opened a dinosaur theme park with huge models overlooking a golf resort. To *say that the public thought that he was eccentric was an understatement. They thought much less of him when he had cashflow issues with his nickel business, owing massive tax debts, making a whole lot of workers redundant with wages, redundancies and leave owed and at the same time heavily investing in his quest to become a political player in federal parliament through his newly formed Palmer United Party. He achieved success in the latter and had to be taken to court over the former issues where he sought continual delays and then somehow negotiated deals that were very much in his favour. His PUP rose like a phoenix in 2013 and he became a member of the House of Representatives along with four others who became senators but two soon left his party because of his dictatorial approach. By the time the 2016 election came the phoenix was in ashes. It rose again in the 2018 and one sitting senator from Pauline Hanson's One Nation party defected to the UAP. In the 2019 election, under the banner of the United Australia Party, Palmer invested \$60 million and succeeded in swaying voters to the conservative side of politics without any of his candidates winning a seat.*

<u>Christopher Pyne</u>

Christopher Pyne came into federal parliament as an MP at the age of 25 in the safe Liberal seat of Sturt. He moved into shadow cabinet in 2008 and when the Coalition came to power in 2013, he became Leader of the House and Minister for Education. He then went on to other ministries before retiring in 2019 having spent 33 years in parliament. He is best known for his dry wit, slightly effeminate voice and for being well liked by all sides of politics. His speed at leaving the chamber when he didn't want to have his vote counted was evident when he and Tony Abbott raced to the doors before they were shut. Christopher proved far too fast for the more athletic Abbott but that was due to his nimble, highly intelligent mind which also left Abbott in its wake.

<u>Kevin Rudd</u>

Kevin Rudd was a Labor leader who had no union affiliations or factions to be beholden to. He had come from the diplomatic corps of the public service and took over as leader of the opposition from the much-liked Kim Beazley in 2006. He took Labor to a landslide win in2007 which saw the sitting Prime Minister, John Howard lose his seat. However, his dictatorial approach to leadership rattled his colleagues and in 2010 Australians woke to find that they had a new PM in Julia Gillard and a new foreign minister in Kevin Rudd. When she looked like facing defeat in 2013 despite having won the 2010 election, she was dumped and Rudd returned as PM in 2013 only to lose the election. Not long after that election Kevin Rudd resigned from parliament. He is best remembered for the apology speech he gave to the indigenous people of Australia and his work in foreign affairs. He remains bitter as to his dumping and regularly adds his voice into the public political discourse.

<u>Bill Shorten</u>

He lost the unlosable election in 2019 because of some very clever campaigning and advertising. As leader of the Opposition for six years until that election he had united the Labor party but hadn't been able to win over the public. His involvement in the removal of Kevin Rudd as PM as well as Julia Gillard as PM didn't help. However, he was a numbers man and had grown up in the union movement and thought he saw the writing on the wall for his party. A Royal Commission into the Union Movement orchestrated by then PM Tony Abbott in an attempt to besmirch Shorten, found no wrongdoing, but it tarnished Shorten's reputation. He is credited with designing the National Disability Insurance Scheme as one of his greatest achievements.

<u>Angus Taylor</u>

The Energy Minister, Angus Taylor has found himself in a lot of hot water. Once seen as future PM material his stocks have fallen low. He has questions to answer on a number of fronts including water buy back schemes where a company he had an interest in made lots of money from the government; doctoring of a document detrimental to the incumbent Sydney Lord Mayor, a position his wife coveted; naming in his maiden speech a well-known author he knew when he was a Rhodes scholar at

Oxford even though she wasn't there at the time; possible unlawful land-clearing on his property. As a strong supporter of coal mining he vigorously defends the government stance on the use/misuse of carbon credits left over from over 20 years before to say that targets will be met.

<u>Malcolm Turnbull</u>

A merchant banker and self-made millionaire, Malcolm Turnbull entered parliament in a blue-ribbon liberal seat and rose through the ranks despite him leading the push for a republic. He played the numbers game after the 2007 election and eventually ousted the newly incumbent leader of the Liberal Party, Brendan Nelson. He was too removed from the job because of his stance on the need for action on climate change, by Tony Abbott. Many years later he would replace Abbot as Prime Minister due to the falling popularity of Abbot. In 2016 he took the government to an election win but was ousted once again because of his climate change stance. He eventually retired from politics and his blue-ribbon seat was taken over by an independent for a short period.

<u>Penny Wong</u>

She is the antithesis of what once was the norm in Australian politics. She is educated, well spoken, surprisingly honest, of Asian extraction and a lesbian. Any of these as well as her gender would see her as the target of political bullying, yet she has risen to Labor's Opposition Leader in the Senate because of her stance over many things including the denigration of women. A strong positive advocate in the Marriage Equality debate, she pulls no punches when she needs to call out bullies, spinners of the truth and outright liars. If she was in the House of Representatives and not the Senate, many believe she would become Australia's second female Prime Minister.

The Overseas Characters

Jacinda Ardern
Boris Johnson
Kim Jong-un
Theresa May
Barack Obama
Xi Jinping
Vladimir Putin
The Royal Family
Donald Trump

Jacinda Ardern

New Zealand's young PM who gave birth while in office, will be remembered for her humanity, stoicism and honesty in really difficult times. She came to world attention after a shooting massacre which ended up with 51 innocent people dying at mosques. Her warmth and sincerity helped heal the country. She was also exceptional when a number of tourists were killed during a volcanic eruption on White Island. Her independence and willingness to speak from the heart at major leadership conferences has been widely acknowledged.

Boris Johnson

Former Lord Mayor of London, Boris Johnson became known as a blond headed fool who sought the limelight, made extravagant promises that he couldn't deliver. Logic said that he was playing well above his capacity and as is the British way, they elected him as PM replacing Theresa May. His rash promises on Brexit and during the election confirming his position may come back to haunt him.

Kim Jong-un

He is the supreme leader of the poor nation of North Korea that has had a succession of leaders all from the one family. Kim Jong-un's rivals from his family seem to mysteriously pass away or disappear. Rather than spend money of feeding the population, Kim Jong-un has spent money on the development of nuclear weapons and ballistic missiles so that he can become a main player on the world stage. He has attracted the attention of China, Japan and the US in particular who have applied trade and other sanctions on North Korea to keep Kim Jong-un in line. Unfortunately, the impact is far more felt on the poor people of North Korea who now have the state-run media telling them that the country is being victimised and oppressed by these countries so North Korea has to fight back. Kim Jong-un seems very artful in wooing attention and exacting promise in return for ones he has no intention of delivering.

Theresa May

May took on the role as PM after the resignation of David Cameron. She had to fight those in her party and those in the Opposition to try to get somewhere in the ongoing saga that was Brexit. Ultimately, she was tossed out by Boris Johnson who said that he had the solution, but has ended up with less than what May had negotiated.

Barack Obama

Spending two terms as president of the US, Barack Obama was the most statesman like president for many years yet it was the downward turning economy that would see his final term being less fruitful. He constantly had to fight battles with the Republican dominated congress and his health care plan that so many poorer Americans would benefit from was a real struggle. In the end a Republican president would dismantle it almost completely.

Xi Jinping

Xi Jinping is the leader of the most highly populated nation in the world and now as President for Life he continues to bring China closer to being the most powerful country in the world. His belt and road policies in poorer countries where he offers infrastructure for influence are getting developing nations on his side. China's expansion into the South China Sea through the creation of artificial islands has caused diplomatic uproar in other nations but Xi Jinping seems unperturbed by that. Rapid expansion has caused difficulties but China is now no longer a developing nation but a major exporter of goods throughout the world. Xi Jinping keeps a close watch over it all and as the companies are largely state run, his leadership decisions are implemented quite quickly and without question. Hong Kong was drawn back into the Chinese control in 1997 and is an essential element of Chinese access to and influence in world trade and affairs. There are major riots occurring in Hong Kong as people are protesting about the crushing of their freedoms. Xi Jinping may be wanting to avoid another Tiananmen Square situation so they haven't been fully crushed as yet.

Vladimir Putin

He took over as President of Russia from Boris Yeltsin in 2000 and through careful swapping of positions with his colleague Dmitry Medvedev (Prime Minister elected in 2000) Putin has led Russia from 2000 through to now. A fitness fanatic and careful diplomat he has improved the circumstances for many of the people in his country whilst still retaining influence in what were states and satellite countries in the old Soviet Union days. Russian military strength is still evident under Putin but also is the use of cyber attacks on countries where Russia now tries to influence election results, most notably the 2016 election in the US. He has often been seen as backing leaderships in countries that are contrary to the ones the US is backing, Syria is a perfect example. This potentially leads to confrontations between the two super powers of Russia and the US and with a diplomatically unstable President Trump in power, the intelligence and guile of Putin in avoiding a conflict has won out so far.

The Royal Family

The royal family began this period with the strange situation where Prince Phillip was given a knighthood by the Australian Prime Minister, Tony Abbott. There have been royal marriages and births as well as scandals involving Prince Andrew and Prince Phillip. The future king's brother, Harry, now married and with a family has asked that he become independent from the throne as another sign that the monarchy is a frail relic that somehow Australia still wishes to cling to.

Donald Trump

Donald Trump was elected president of the United States in 2016 despite his strange behaviour. He defeated Hilary Clinton after bullying and intimidation and a smear campaign. He somehow managed to do the same thing to other Republican candidates and win the candidacy and then the presidency. He has had a high rotation of staff and has put out fake news and uses twitter to state new policies. After seeming to threaten Ukraine with blackmail in order to get information on his own potential opponent he eventually was impeached by the House. He has been continually mocked by world leaders and has met with the president of North Korea among others in what now appears to be a waste of time. He has withdrawn troops from the Middle East leaving the countries there open for more warfare. He has also pulled out of climate change agreements, trade agreements and nuclear agreements. Lacking diplomacy, economic vision and the ability to communicate with women in particular, he has walked the world stage with the world half in fear that the ignorant spoilt brat of a buffoon may one day begin a nuclear war simply because he can.

The Issues

Asylum seekers/Immigration
Banking
Border Protection
Brexit
Bushfires
China
Climate change
Defence
Drought
The economy
Education
Elections
Environment
First Australians
Leadership
Marriage Equality/Gender Equity
The Media
Middle East
North Korea
Religious Freedoms
Russia
Unemployment/Employment
Unions
World trade

Asylum seekers/Immigration

Australia has had a major issue with asylum seekers. It has taken over five years before so many of them have been processed. They are incarcerated in concentration type camps in foreign countries including on Nauru and Manus Island. These camps have been funded for by Australia but Australia claims no responsibility. It seems it is an out of sight, out of mind policy that is being enacted. At the end of 2018 moves were afoot to allow asylum seekers trapped in concentration camp type conditions to be assessed by independent doctors and if treatment was needed, they were to be transferred to Australia. This was successful but quickly repealed after the May 2019 election.

Banking

The Australian economy remains reliant on the four-pillar banking system. Four privately owned banks, two of which were once owned by the government, remain dominant and the government seems to be at their beck and call. In the Global Financial Crisis of 2007-2008, the government was forced to underwrite these banks because the banks were so intrinsically part of the economy that if one or more failed the nation would fail. These banks because of their size, power and reach were often seen to be making their own rules. After years of being asked, the Coalition finally called a Royal Commission into the banking sector and the rorts were revealed. However, it seems little has changed.

Border Protection

The Australian government dramatically beefed up its border protection after 2013. Special units of armed "Border Force" personnel were formed and some government departments and spy agencies were melded into one super ministry called Home Affairs with special powers and controlled by one minister, Peter Dutton. Australia had gone from a friendly welcoming place to what some people described as a police state. Freedoms were slowly being eroded, including those of the media.

Brexit

In 2016 There was a referendum in Britain about whether Britain should leave the European Union. The Leave vote was heavily reliant on the push factor of immigration and the loss of jobs and didn't really discuss the consequences of such a departure. The Prime Minister David Cameron resigned when the Brexit result was announced. Theresa May was appointed his replacement and set about working through all the conditions to achieve a Brexit deal and avoid some of the ramifications. In the end it cost her her job and she was replaced with Boris Johnson who called an immediate election to ensure that he had the country's backing. Postponement after postponement had taken place since the referendum but a final date was set when a whole new set of border and economic problems would change Britain forever and perhaps disunite the United Kingdom completely as Northern Ireland and Scotland voted to stay in the European Community.

<u>Bushfires</u>

Australia's climate continues to change for the worse. We have always been a place of 'drought and flooding rain'. After years of drought, massive bushfires hit Australia in the last months of 2019 and the early months of 2020 killing many, destroying homes, livestock, forests and wildlife. Many parts of the whole east coast, parts of Tasmania, South Australia and Western Australia were ablaze and attracted worldwide attention and support. Prime Minister Scott Morrison was loudly and strongly condemned for taking a family holiday during that time and not providing the leadership required. Firefighters, mostly volunteers had not had a break for months because the fires were so severe and were unable to be put out. The navy stepped in and rescued people in isolated towns who had fled to the beaches trying to survive. Months and years before government bodies had asked for more money to buy more equipment but the government had denied their request.

China

China's rise to power as a nation has had major implications on trade with Australia and on its diplomatic defence strategies. It is a major importer of our minerals, especially coal, which China consumes 13% of our exports. We, in turn, import 25% of our goods from China. Australia also provides many opportunities in its universities for Chinese students. Concern has been expressed over the purchase of properties, businesses and opportunities by China in Australia and also China's expansion into the South China Sea. There are also signs that politicians have been influenced by Chinese 'gifts'. Senator Sam Dastyari was forced to resign over his links with Chinese moneylenders. At the moment Australia is caught in the middle of a trade war between the US which sees itself as the leader of the world, and the upwardly moving China that will soon dislodge it. Defence ties with the US and trade ties with China make for awkward negotiations for Australian diplomats and politicians especially as the state-owned Chinese company Huawei wish to become involved in the expansion of Australia's telecommunication network.

<u>Climate change</u>

The vast majority of the population acknowledges that there is global warming caused by increased carbon in the atmosphere and that man through its use of fossil fuels contributes heavily to that carbon. There are people in parliament in Australia who deny such things and are at the beck and call of the mining industry. These same right-wing people have controlled any possible position that the Australian government can take to reduce the emissions. Twice Malcolm Turnbull has lost his position because of it, one when he was Prime Minister. Kevin Rudd and Julia Gillard both lost their Prime Ministerships because of the stance and Tony Abbott rose to power because of it. The Coalition government, with a wafer-thin majority could lose power if some of the ultra conservatives withdraw their support. It is a case of a few controlling the vast majority and Australia and the world suffers because of it.

<u>Defence</u>

Australia relies heavily on the US alliances for defence. This has led us into wars however including Vietnam, two Iraqi wars, Afghanistan and against ISIS. The country spends about 2% GDP on defence. In 2020 this is about $40 billion. Very little equipment is made in Australia and our once great shipyards and other defence industries are just shadows of what they used to be. Major contracts have been signed for submarines and planes that will be delivered many years in the future and possibly by then will be out of date and inferior. For many average Australians who see the photo ops of politicians doing their big boys and their toys routine, the expenditure seems unwarranted and money would be better spent on the homeless, reducing the crippling debt that we have. The military in peace time have done us proud in East Timor and assisting with recovery in disaster situations. They remain independent of the government and the Prime Minister is not the Commander in Chief.

<u>Drought</u>

Australia has been enduring more frequent drought periods of late. They are more widespread, lasting longer and having a bigger impact on the country's ability to grow sustainable crops and to farm traditional livestock. There is a growing belief that the foodbowl that we once were, is becoming a thing of the past. Changing away from traditional methods and recognising that there is a water shortage may help stem the flow of farm foreclosures, farmer suicides and small towns shutting up shops. There are rorts in the Murray Darling water catchment and water allocation. Those downstream suffer the most. Droughts are linked to climate change and the federal government has been slow to act. They are more likely to pout an ambulance at the bottom of a cliff than fence off the top of the cliff.

<u>The economy</u>

Australia has a preoccupation with the economy and that drives policy more than the needs of people. We have ever mounting debt and our GDP has fallen because we rely heavily on mining. Our manufacturing industry has all but stalled. Low wage growth, excessive government spending and poorly funded community service programs like aged pension, unemployment benefits and disability and aged care sectors, mean that the people who need help the most become the first casualties of a stagnant economy.

<u>Education</u>

Australian runs a private and state-run school system. The state-run one is supposed to be free and secular, but that is a matter of debate. By comparison the state-run system is poorly funded compared with the private one as federal government funding flows fairly freely to the private system. This has a real bearing on the social strata that lies under the surface of the egalitarian life that Australians believe they have. Introduction of and publication of testing across schools has not properly assessed student outcomes and instead has set up competition between schools and widened the divide between rich and poor schools both in the private and state-run system. Religious groups such as Catholics run separate schools in the private/independent system and are heavily reliant on federal funding. Come election times, whichever party is in power, school funding is used to benefit the party and its ideology. All schools are having less time to do their basic work as more and more of society's ills are blamed on the school system and schools are forced to add "fix-ups" into their curriculum.

Elections

Australians seemed to have a revolving door of Prime Ministers from 2007 onwards. Four times the Prime Ministership was changed without an election. This was very destabilising. After one merry go round ride of Prime Ministers, Tony Abbott swept to power in 2013 only to be part of a domino chain of Prime Ministers leading to Scott Morrison thrust into the position just before an election. He won the unwinnable election by one seat. Many of his counterparts left parliament altogether choosing not to stand rather than lose their seat.

Environment

Australia has a unique environment. It is extremely fragile however and for centuries the indigenous population have managed it. Within the last two centuries since the arrival of Europeans and their land and marine management, there have been massive changes, most of them negative. Entire species of animals have been wiped out and native vegetation has been lost. Heralded all around the world is our Great Barrier Reef but the global warming that has changed the temperature of the water, the use of fertilisers that get washed downstream into the ocean and the introduction of non-native species such as the crown of thorns starfish have decimated a large extent of the reef. Tourism has suffered accordingly. The Reef is a prime example of what is happening across Australia. The Greens political party was set up to provide arguments for a better awareness and management of the environment but they have become just another party, but one of the far left. The public are often left with the feeling of helplessness as the people they elect don't seem to care because the economy is seen to be more important than the environment. Melissa Price was appointed Environment minister by Scott Morrison but had no qualifications apart from a mining background. She made many gaffes and went MIA around election time in 2019.

First Australians

When the Europeans arrived in Australia, they declared the land Terra Nullis indicating that no-one lived there. In doing so, they were stating that the indigenous population were nothing more than fauna, which also meant that the Europeans effectively stole the land from those who had come before them. No treaty such as the one in New Zealand was ever signed. Aborigines became slaves, were conscripted into the army, had their children taken from them to be raised "properly" and were given very few benefits and moved out of productive land. In 1967 they were finally given the right to vote. Under a Labor government in the 1970's they were also allowed to argue for their land rights. For a long period under a conservative government there was little progress made. In 2008 they were finally given a much belated apology about the stolen generation (children taken from their families). In 2017, the celebrated Statement from the Heart was made recommending changes to the way the indigenous population could have a voice about their future. The Coalition government rejected it out of hand.

Leadership

Australia had been devoid of strong leadership since around 1996 in the early days of John Howards prime ministership both in opposition and government at a federal level. The state governments had a number of effective progressive leaders in that time but there was not the quality coming through at a federal level who were willing and capable of leading. Some were trapped in the senate and couldn't become a prime minister. With so many factions in the major parties, would be leaders needed to spend more time unifying their party than unifying the nation. Oppositions and governments were at loggerheads just to prove that there was a point of difference. The image of politicians and indeed leaders went on a downward spiral and may not have bottomed out yet.

Marriage Equality/Gender Equity

The idea that LGBTQI people should be able to legally marry had been the bone of contention for a long long time. Some states wished to make it happen but were wary because the federal government had power to override state laws. It was determined that a law had to be enacted federally to guarantee people the rights that others took for granted. There were all sorts of delaying mechanisms put in place by right wing parliamentarians, media shock jocks and by religious groups. One of these was the introduction of a plebiscite which was a very expensive, non-binding and unnecessary act to slow down the momentum. It was very divisive, yet in the end proved to the politicians that the vast majority of Australians wanted marriage equality to happen. The passing of the law on Marriage Equality was celebrated by LGBTQI and heterosexuals alike and the ultra-conservative politicians when asked to vote in parliament defied their constituents by abstaining or voting no. They proved to be only a minority.

<u>The Media</u>

The media in Australia used to be quite diverse and rules were put in place so that no one person or media company could dominate. However, under changes by the Coalition these rules were relaxed and the Newscorp companies have begun to dominate print, radio and television media, squeezing out the smaller players. The owners of large media companies have extraordinary access to and influence on politicians and policies of parties. Rupert Murdoch is one of the owners who has more say than most. Politicians have been stretching "in confidence" aspects of the law to stop or delay Freedom of Information requests by journalists and when information has been released it has often been heavily redacted. Pressure has been placed on journalists and media groups to reveal sources through the use of Federal Police. Politicians however use the media for the purpose of deliberately leaking of information and have become very fussy whom they will be interviewed by on radio and television. Door stop interviews to create sound bites suitable for the evening news are often held but politicians are finding it difficult to adapt to the 24-hour news cycle and the rise of social media.

<u>Middle East</u>

The Middle East has been a hot bed of uncertainty and division from the earliest of times, some of it religious based, most of it economic. With the rise of the need for oil products, it became and remains a powder keg. At the end of World War 1 artificial lines were drawn on a map separating tribes and families. At the end of the Second World War there was a need to create a Jewish state and the nation of Israel further divided the area. War after war has been fought non-stop between a host of nations. Interference by multinationals and backed by European and US governments has not helped. The ever-present threat of a nuclear holocaust exists and when one renegade Arab group took on the US on US soil causing the 9/11 events, the world held its collective breath. Strategic withdrawal of US European and Russian troops seems unlikely as this led to the rise of other groups such as Al-Qaeda and ISIS. Underlying all this is the world's need for petroleum-based products.

<u>North Korea</u>

This poor impoverished reclusive nation has been under the rule of one family since 1948. Money is spent on developing nuclear capabilities and missiles to strike countries. Surrounded by China, Russia and South Korea, its leaders have been able to get the population to believe that they are under imminent attack. Widely seen as a renegade state, it manages to strut a high profile and threaten countries around it.

<u>Religious Freedoms</u>

Australia has a good set of discrimination laws despite it not actually having a bill of rights. After the religious community were rolled in the Marriage Equality discussion, plebiscite and vote, voices were raised about enshrining discriminatory rights for religions into law. Australia is supposed to have a separation between church and state, through secular governments. This is more in name than in deed as the religious lobby groups wield a lot of power and influence despite a steep decline in the number of people practising any religion. The Coalition government has been pushing for a revamp of the religious discrimination laws to allow religious bodies to have special dispensation to discriminate.

<u>Russia</u>

Since the end of the Cold War in 1991, Russia has loomed large in Australia's foreign affairs as Australia walks a tightrope of increasing its trade with Russia but also aware of Russia's expansion plans through influencing other countries. Tony Abbott once threatened to "shirtfront" Vladimir Putin over Russian involvement in the downing of a plane and its use naval ships north of Australia. Abbott had no idea what shirtfront really meant. Putin laughed it off and Australia went down in Russian estimation. Because of our close defence ties with the US, Australia has often been drawn into issues that involve Russia.

<u>Unemployment/Employment</u>

Financial support for those unemployed has waned and many people are struggling. Rules on statistics have been changed and there is a steady increase in the underemployed. With a stroke of a pen, someone working one hour per week is considered employed. Newstart is an allowance given to the unemployed to support them when seeking new jobs. Those on these benefits must be actively seeking employment, even if there is none or they lose the benefits. They become easy targets for politicians and the media and named as dole bludgers. For many people particularly in rural regions there aren't jobs available and this causes an exodus to the city as it is difficult to survive on the allowance given. Australian manufacturing has all but shut down completely. There is a large amount of automation in many work places and that means that fewer people are needed. With a large pool of people to choose from, employers are able to suppress wages too. Traditional jobs gone, little change in education to expand opportunities, low wage growth and a very low unemployment benefit, young people cannot get into the job market and housing market. This just further stagnates the economy.

<u>Unions</u>

There has been a dramatic decline in union membership in Australia to the extent that the Labor Party, the traditional voice of the unions in parliament are losing their base and are being forced to look elsewhere. Many unions have become political and dominated by trying to achieve political ideological gains rather than act in the best interest of their members. This has led to the disenfranchisement of members and the loss of membership. However, the biggest change has been due to the Coalition government's push to undermine unions and change labour laws.

World trade

Countries and groups of nations have put in trade tariffs and barriers to protect their own producers. However, because there is a supply and demand backbone to all their economies, and multinational companies, governments have been trying to reach individual agreements between countries. Some of these are symbolic and trade can see the dumping of cheap or excess products which greatly affect an individual nation. Cheap labour in some countries undercuts others. Scarcity of one commodity can affect the capacity of another. There is no level playing field as countries try to woo individual companies with lucrative tax deals. China has entered the market and is now a powerful player and the once dominant US is finding it difficult to lose its stranglehold on world markets.

Return to Contents page